GOD @ GROUND ZERO

GOD @ GROUND ZERO

How Good Overcame Evil . . . One Heart at a Time

"CHAPLAIN RAY" GIUNTA

with Lynda Rutledge Stephenson

INTEGRITY®

PUBLISHERS

Nashville

GOD @ GROUND ZERO

Published in association with Yates and Yates, LLP, Literary Agents,
Orange, California.

Cover Design: David Uttley
Interior Design: Inside Out Design & Typesetting

ISBN 1-59145-015-2

Printed in the United States of America
02 03 04 05 06 BP 9 8 7 6 5 4 3 2 1

Contents

CONTENTS

Acknowledgments

THE CREATION OF THIS BOOK could only have happened through a small miracle of help from a host of remarkable people. My wife, Cathy, and my terrific kids, Kimberlee, Kyle, and Katie, head the list. Allowing me to be away from home so much during times of disaster was a big sacrifice for them, and I felt their love and support every day and every step of this journey.

Special thanks to my ministry partners, Reverend Jeff Jones and Robert Dail Sr., for supporting the vision of We Care Ministries with their prayers and faithfulness. Thanks also to our financial supporters: to A. Teichert & Son and every one of its great employees, to our friends at Macy's and Svenhard's Bakery, to the students and faculty at Capital Christian School, and to those churches who have given graciously to this ministry.

Thanks to my mom and dad, Frank and Rose Giunta, for taking in a stray and providing unconditional love and a wonderful home. Thanks also to my brothers and sisters, each one of whom is special and will forever be in my heart. My heartfelt appreciation also goes out to all the volunteer chaplains who have faithfully answered the call to action in times of crisis with us,

ACKNOWLEDGMENTS

including Bob, Tim, John, Bart, Jim, Kevin, Leah, Andrew, Rob, Mary Grace, Gary, Ryan, Bob, Sealy, Max, Diane, Martha, and Anthony. I'm also grateful to the hundreds of others too numerous to name with whom we've had the privilege of working, including all the relief workers at ground zero, as well as the workers at other "ground zero" experiences, large and small, throughout the years.

A special thanks to Integrity Publishers, to Byron, Joey, Rob, and Sue Ann for believing in this project and for guiding it into book form.

To Lynda Rutledge Stephenson I express deepest thanks for helping me shape my indescribable experiences at ground zero into the meaningful story I wanted to tell but didn't know how.

And thanks to God for the opportunity We Care was given to serve during these historic disasters, as well as for the gift of Himself in Christ, our deepest answer in times of crisis.

PROLOGUE

Where Was God?

I HAD JUST FINISHED C-WATCH, *the night shift, working along-side firefighters at ground zero all night long. The sun had just come up. Ahead of me, I saw someone leaning on a piece of construction equipment. It was a woman in her thirties. She was wearing jeans and a detective's badge, but I still thought her being there at that time of day was odd. It had been a cold and rainy night. The sunlight had just come through the buildings, and it was shining on her face in a golden way. She was soaking it in, sitting all by herself.*

Her name was Beth. I asked, "Where were you when this happened?"

"Right here," she said, "working in a triage area we'd set up. There were firefighters here with us, and we were all helping people who'd been hurt when the planes crashed into the towers." She paused, looking past me. "Until the building came down."

The force of the implosion blew her thirty yards, into a revolving door, along with two firefighters who had instinctively covered her with their own bodies an instant before the blast. Everyone else near her in the triage area, she told me, was somewhere under the collapsed building.

She had come every day since the attack, always to the same spot, always at the same time, trying to make sense of the senseless. "Why did I live?" she asked. "Those people standing right by me . . . what about them? Why did God let this happen?"

The World Trade Center disaster was different from other crisis events I had faced in this one unique aspect: Spiritual questions were in the air as much as the World Trade Center's dust. I had seen nothing like it in all my years of crisis work. Every conversation included this kind of dialogue—on the subway, along the ground zero site perimeter, on the sidewalks, in the relief centers, on the ferry, in the moonlight and the dust-filled sunshine. It flowed naturally and urgently. And the heart of each encounter was the age-old question asked in the aftermath of every atrocity of history: Where was God?

Throughout all I've seen in this work, all the things I've heard, and all the things I trust, there has always been one belief I rest in. It is what allows me to keep doing this work, no matter how grim it becomes. And that belief, I realized, was what would give Beth the comfort she needed.

I told her where I believed God was during this disaster . . .

Chapter One

The Language of the Day

Today, as I write this, reflecting on all the days and nights I spent in New York City in the aftermath of September 11, hundreds of moments, images, and faces float to the front of my mind. I want to make sense of it all, even though I know that will never fully happen.

And yet . . .

There are days in life that you recognize, without doubt, as turning points. Life lessons are learned in the wake of such extraordinary moments. They become our defining stories, the ones we tell for the rest of our lives because we know they somehow hold insight into life's meaning.

I have three such days. And, as if to make sure I never forget them, they all came attached to newspaper headlines.

December 6, 1987, headline:

BIRTHDAY RIDE TURNS INTO

TRAGEDY FOR TWO SMALL FRIENDS

I was twenty-seven years old. I had left a career in law enforcement to become a minister. But I was impatient with the

1

day-to-day business of church work. That morning, I made the
mistake of reading the newspaper. On the front page was the
story of two little boys who had been celebrating one of the boy's
birthdays by riding around together on a Big Wheel tricycle.
When they pedaled down their apartment building's driveway
and into the street, a car had hit them, dragging them a
hundred yards and killing them. Both were children of single
mothers who were now facing the worst crisis a parent can
experience.

Who was helping these people? I wondered. I told my secretary I couldn't work that day, and left to investigate. When I
arrived at the apartments, I walked past the yellow police tape
around the crime scene and into my future.

That moment had been a long time coming. Now I can see,
with the clarity of hindsight, that the decision had been a direct
result of two earlier days—twenty-five years apart:

Easter Sunday, March 30, 1986, headline:
SIBLINGS ABANDONED IN 1961 REUNITED

Everything had begun just before my first child's birth. I was still
working for the state of California as a criminal investigator. As a
matter of routine, my wife's obstetrician had requested both our
families' medical histories. Yet I couldn't offer anything. I had
been adopted; I didn't know my birth family, much less my
parents' medical pasts. My wife urged me to investigate the
matter. I was hesitant, but for my baby daughter's sake, I made one

attempt. And with one phone call, an all-but-miraculous chain of events was put into motion that led me back to a Ray I had never known. My unknown past, my fall into a childhood act of grace, unfolded before me.

October 17, 1961, headline:
MOTHER HUNTED FOR DESERTION OF 9 KIDS

The child of a welfare mother and a father in prison for failure to support his family, I was the youngest of nine children born within ten years. One day when I was ten months old, my mother went out for bread and never came home. A week passed before social services discovered all of us, dirty and hungry. They found me in an open bureau drawer near death.

The details stunned me. My sisters and brothers had been scattered into foster care, most of them enduring hardships that I could not imagine. During Easter week, 1986, following that one phone call, we would all find each other again after a quarter of a century. And the story would make national news.

Discovering the existence of an alternate life, a whole other Ray, was a personal revelation, to say the least. I should never have survived, much less flourished. From the day of that discovery forward, I unconsciously began a soul search that, in 1987, led me through that yellow police tape and into a career working in compassionate crisis care. The child of crisis would choose to spend his life working with other people's crises.

In the next fourteen years of meeting the needs of victims

traumatized by both local and national disasters—from 911 calls to school shootings, from earthquakes to domestic terrorist bombings—I would see and hear everything. Or so I thought.

Of all people, I should have learned never to be surprised where life leads. Because now it seems to me that the headline moments I had experienced were only a prologue for another turning-point headline day, for me and for an entire nation:

September 11, 2001 headline:
TERRORISTS ATTACK WORLD TRADE CENTER

I learned about the terrorist attack on September 11 the way most Americans did—progressively.

On my way to a 6 A. M. meeting in Sacramento, California, I overheard someone say, "A plane just hit the World Trade Center."

A few minutes later, I heard the same news again. Or so it seemed.

"No, no, another one hit!"

Another one? I thought.

Then, as the meeting began, someone burst into the room and said, "The Pentagon has just been attacked by a plane. The country's at war!"

We turned on the nearest television to see the plane-crash footage that would soon be seared into an entire nation's consciousness. In the hours ahead, I joined the rest of America, listening and watching, as the media began its race for the news.

Television had never been so powerful; we were seeing a

terrorist attack, and we were seeing it live. With each minute that passed after the first plane hit at 8:46 eastern daylight time, more and more people turned on their televisions. From shore to shore, around the globe and back, no one seemed spared. It was coming at us, into our vision, into our psyches, shaking us to our very beings. We had believed we were safe and would always be. It was a stunning loss of innocence, gone for good.

The East Coast attacks had occurred at the start of the workday. So those of us on the West Coast began to dread the ticks of the clock as it neared 9 A. M. California time. The position and number of the hijacked planes were still in doubt. When the moment came, we braced for news from San Francisco, Los Angeles, or San Diego. Thankfully, none came. Yet I recall feeling no relief, only a sort of readiness for the trauma wave to come, the kind I'd felt before each crisis I'd experienced. The magnitude of this event was going to be unique. Sadly, we were all casualties of this attack. The instant quality of television spontaneously created a nation of victims. This would be the first time since the Kennedy assassination that the national networks preempted all programming for such an extended period in order to show news of one event. The news coverage would go on nonstop for four days. Whether we watched it live via television feeds, saw its videotape replayed incessantly, or read about it in detailed newspaper accounts, we were collectively traumatized and we would collectively grieve. I recognized the dynamic, but I was as unprepared as the rest of the country for the scope of the impact.

As the day progressed, I called my We Care Ministries partner, Jeff Jones. We had fourteen years' experience in crisis intervention work, providing counseling and assistance to victims of trauma. I stated what we were both thinking:

"I think we'll probably go to New York."

"Yeah, I think so, too," he agreed.

"Let's just see what happens," I added.

Since we had so much hands-on experience, I felt, right from the disaster's first moments, that we should go; but I had learned to wait. If God wanted us to go, we'd go. Something would open up. If God didn't want us to go, then we would not. Such a thing I don't say lightly, yet I've come to trust it. Our basic philosophy has always been that we only respond to a crisis if we are invited by some institution or group. Our simplest rule was to wait until we received a call, some connection, before we blustered into a disaster site's chaos. That was our own checks-and-balances system, our way of being sure we were supposed to go. We'd seen far too many individuals and groups show up at disaster sites only to become more of a hindrance than a help due to their having no specific connection.

But at that time, we couldn't travel anyway; all commercial airlines were grounded. If we were to go quickly, we would have to catch a military flight, and very few of those were flying, either. In the past, we had flown with the Federal Emergency Management Agency's urban search and rescue field team based in Sacramento, with whom we'd worked during the 1995 Oklahoma City bombing disaster. However, they were in a hold mode as well, awaiting orders. The FEMA team's chaplain asked us to be on call, to stand ready.

As another day passed, though, it occurred to me that maybe we wouldn't be going. Beyond the strong desire we felt to be "there," the event was also happening "here."

More and more people in Sacramento had begun to ask for help. They couldn't focus at their desks. They couldn't concentrate on their work; they were afraid for their children. They were afraid for the future. So we began to work at home, counseling clients about a terrorist attack we all had experienced via television. The demand for crisis training and counseling at home was so great, Jeff and I realized that one of us should stay even if an invitation did materialize to go to New York. We were also not convinced that the West Coast was beyond the possibility of attack. So we decided that Jeff would stay in California, either way, to direct We Care's work there. In the weeks ahead, among other things, he'd arrange a symposium of crisis experts from the Red Cross, Salvation Army, and police and fire chaplaincy.

A couple more days went by. As we worked at home, we kept up with everything happening at the World Trade Center area now being called poignantly "ground zero." The site was pure chaos. The nation's expertise in responding to disasters had matured along with ever-succeeding events—a sad indictment of modern life—but this one was beyond comprehension for even the most expert forces. In Oklahoma City, among the elite USAR (urban search and rescue) teams with whom we'd worked was one from New York led by a well-known New York firefighter named

Ray Downey. News filtered out to us that many of those team members, Downey most conspicuously, were missing after the Twin Towers' collapse. I felt more than ever we could help after hearing such terrible news.

I called Jeff.

"I really feel like we need to go. Our bags are packed," I said. "But we need to have someone ask us to come."

What wasn't being said was obvious: *Should we break our rule?*

"Let's wait a little longer," Jeff said.

I hung up the phone.

And it immediately rang. A San Jose friend was calling to say he had been in contact with a Manhattan pastor whose church, within blocks of ground zero, was swamped with needs. And he had asked for our help.

I grabbed my bag.

THE CLOSEST DEPARTURE POINT FOR the first direct flight to New York was Las Vegas, so two other team members and I caught a crack-of-dawn commuter flight to Las Vegas from the Sacramento airport. At the Las Vegas airport, though, we were in for a surprise. We weren't prepared for how much our whole world had changed. We were wearing our tactical, police-style blue uniforms, along with clerical collars that identified us as chaplains. I had gotten used to people calling me "father" because of the collar, even though I wasn't a priest. If I could help someone, they could call me anything they wanted, especially if it made me "safe" to approach. So, even if my Protestant denomination did not use collars, I would wear one during crisis work anyway. I had learned from experience how important such symbols are.

In the very height of a crisis, denominational lines, even religious lines, are irrelevant. What we represent for the needy is most important, and being easily recognized is everything. Visible cues such as crosses on our blue uniforms, clerical collars around our necks, and hard hats bearing crosses do exactly that. Those of us who wear such symbols are the ones who pick up the pieces after a tragedy, the ones who bury the dead and pray for the victims, but the symbols also seem to provide another message. I've noticed that they offer a silent, simple witness to something incredibly comforting. The crosses and the clerical collars seem to be quiet reminders of hope, of divine presence, that God is still there in the midst of tragedy. Just to see the symbol of the cross is to be reminded of Christ's love. And that dynamic helps us as well; we don't have to say much, if anything at all, to still help in this special way. Often, these symbols alone can offer what people need.

All eyes turned our way as we moved through the Las Vegas terminal, just as they had in the Sacramento airport. In the predawn hours in Sacramento, though, no one had approached us, and the looks we received had seemed full of sudden sadness. It was as if the sight of chaplains in uniforms was yet another grim reality check—a full recognition that people had died. But in Las Vegas, the story would be dramatically different.

"God bless ya!" we heard someone yell.

I turned to see an elderly black man shining a businessman's shoes and smiling at me—at the same time. The moment was almost awkward.

"Well, God bless you, too," I said.

"Oh, every day. The Lord and I, we're blessing people coming and going." His name was J. J., he said. "Where're you going?"

"New York," I said.

"Oh, dear Lord, I can't even believe it. Let's just pray right now," he said.

So, right there in the Las Vegas airport, J. J. and I had a moment of prayer while the businessman waited to have his other shoe shined.

At that moment, I began to grasp just how different this trip was going to be.

Our flight was delayed, as most flights were during that week. So we sat down in an airport restaurant to wait. A woman approached us. She was obviously of East Indian descent, Iranian or Pakistani, and she was wearing a shawl of the kind women wore in the Muslim world.

"Can you hold my bag?" she asked.

My first thought was, *This is an airport! How could I possibly hold this woman's bag?* To make me even more nervous, the bag looked like a diaper bag—but I didn't see a diaper, and I didn't see a baby.

I didn't like this at all.

"Why do you want me to hold your bag?" I asked.

"Oh . . . I want to go to the restroom, and I want to get something to eat . . . and, well . . ." She was barely coherent.

"It's a very small bag. Why can't you carry it with you?" I tried.

"I . . . don't know . . ."

"Ma'am," I finally said. "You're really not making sense. There's just been a terrorist attack, and you're asking a stranger in an airport to hold your carry-on."

She looked even more confused.

"Where are you going?" one of my team members asked her.

"Austin," she answered. "Where are you going?"

"New York," he answered.

"Oh, really . . . I'm a psychologist; I should probably be going to New York, too."

"Why don't you?" I said.

She suddenly began to weep.

Then I realized that was the reason this Muslim woman had approached us. We were safe. And this country must have felt anything but safe to her at that moment. The bag wasn't why she was standing in front of us. It was only an excuse to connect with three safe men who were wearing clerical collars. Within a few seconds, we were praying again, this time to help her travel with courage. It was another simple prayer in the middle of the Las Vegas airport.

Prayer in the middle of an airport was suddenly not so unusual. Prayer in the restroom wouldn't have been unusual. Almost every encounter would include a prayer. It would be even truer in New York City. Prayer in supermarkets, train stations, and bus stations would become a natural occurrence.

As we went toward our gate, we were stopped in our tracks, over and over again, to be asked for prayer. The need to be connected was overpowering. Watching the events on television at home was traumatic enough, but to be in an airport, where the disaster had begun only a week earlier, was troubling us all.

Every few steps, it seemed, someone was either touching us or asking for a prayer. As I walked, passersby would put their hands on my arm. "God bless you," many would say, and we'd return the blessing.

"Will you pray with me? Can you do that here?"

"That's what we do," I'd respond. In truth, it was what I'd been doing since hearing of the tragedy, talking to God, minute by minute—*Should we go, how will we get there, who will we serve, what will be our assignment?* Prayer had been talking, asking, listening, and waiting. Then, as we were on our way, prayer became practical demonstrations of faith—prayer for peace, prayer for comfort, prayer for protection, prayer for a nation under siege. But most of all, prayer was another reminder of spiritual presence. That is always what it has been for me, but for those in crisis, that reminder is especially significant. Social work brings compassion; education brings knowledge; prayer brings God's presence, leaving those who've participated in it with hope and peace beyond human understanding.

So, personal public prayer is a normal thing in crisis work. In some parts of the country it is not only natural but expected—throughout the Bible Belt, for instance, which was the case after the Oklahoma City bombing. But for it also to be true in Las

Vegas and, soon, in New York City would speak volumes. People did not have a vocabulary for what they were feeling, so prayer had become a common language beyond faiths, genders, or socioeconomic classes. Prayer became the medication of the soul, the very breath of life, the language of the day.

AS WE BOARDED THE PLANE, the tension was thick. It was the same story for travelers across the nation, if not the world, since the unfolding stories from the doomed planes were now common knowledge. We all wondered who our fellow passengers were, what they were carrying onto the plane, and who was in charge.

One of the flight attendants quietly said to me as we boarded, "You don't know what it means for us to have you on board." Another one told me there were now two groups of people they all loved having on their flights: pilots who know how to fly the plane and official people of faith. They wanted around them rescuers in a physical sense and in a spiritual sense as well. It was so powerful and humbling.

The looks we were receiving from passengers as we boarded in our uniforms and clergy collars were a mixture of everything we were all feeling.

We settled into our seats. The plane was half-empty.

As soon as we were airborne, I had an overwhelming urge to get out of my seat and talk to people. From my experience, that was what made all the difference in the wake of crisis—talking. But I knew asking to use the airplane's microphone was not only out of the question considering the hijackings but certainly the quickest way to be arrested—not to mention scaring the heck out of everyone, the very opposite of what I felt I was being led to accomplish.

So I thought, *Okay, now what am I supposed to do?*

I asked the airline attendant about the idea. "What do you think about my talking to the passengers, maybe offering to visit with each of them for a few minutes?"

"Oh, take your liberty, do whatever you want to do," she said. "Even when the seatbelt sign is lit, you have permission to move around. Just be careful if we hit some bumps."

I didn't want to scare people, though, I explained.

"Why don't you start at the back?" she suggested. "That might help."

So I did. In normal times, there is a wall that goes up between strangers, even when they're jammed together on airplanes. And rightly so. But, as I suspected, times not being normal, everyone wanted to talk.

So, as I moved down the aisle, I introduced myself to many of the passengers, and if there was a vacant seat, I sat down beside them. "Hi, I'm Chaplain Ray, and I'm going to New York to help," I would say. "But before I get there, I was wondering if I could help you? How are you doing since the attack? What's going on for you right now?"

I found out who my fellow passengers were and heard their

personal dramas. Two were even connected to the attack. A man named Tom had been in the World Trade Center, on the seventieth floor of Tower One, the north tower. The first plane had hit the north tower at the ninety-third floor.

"When I made it out of the building," he told me, "I kept going. I left New York the same day. I got in a car and just drove as far as I could. I was a mess. I had to get out of there. So I drove all the way to Las Vegas. Now I'm going back for the first time."

"What was it like leaving a building that had just been hit by an airplane?" I asked him.

"There was an urgency to get out, but people were all being polite as we worked our way down. No one truly knew the extent of the attack, or even if it was an attack." The lights had gone out when he heard the crash, then emergency lighting flickered on. He began to wonder if it had been a bomb. For twenty minutes, he and his co-workers had descended, going down, down, down the stairwells, as doors from each floor swung open and more people joined the throng. That's when he saw the fire for the first time and the first people suffering from burns and shock. "We had no idea what was about to happen." As he had stepped into a dark lobby, he heard another explosion, and glass shattered all around him as he ran for the exit. "The buildings collapsed after everyone going down with me was out, but there were lots of people behind me."

"What stays with you the most?" I asked.

"Their faces. I'll never forget their faces."

"Whose faces?"

"The firefighters'," he said. "As we hit the thirty-fifth floor going down, I saw them coming up. They were exhausted, panting, out of breath. I saw them; they saw me. I went down. They kept going up."

"Do you know if they got out?"

He said, "I don't know. But their faces will be with me forever."

A young couple was from the Washington, D.C., area. They had felt the same way after the Pentagon attack so close to their home. They had flown to Las Vegas as soon as it was possible, just to get away from the fear of more attacks. Now they were having to face the reality of returning home.

Other stories were intensely personal. One man said he was going to Albany, New York, where his mother was dying of cancer. "We're going to unplug the machine when I get there."

Another man, a pilot, was flying to his father's funeral. He had a Bible in his lap. "I have to do the service, and I've never done a service before," he told me.

"I've done many services," I said. "Maybe I could help you."

We planned his father's funeral service, sitting there on the plane.

All the passengers I met seemed to be deep into their own dramas. Perhaps that would be true of any group on an airplane flight if passengers shared the stories they were carrying with them, but against the backdrop of September 11, each story held an extra poignancy.

THAT EVENING, SEPTEMBER 17, WE landed at Islip, the Long Island airport near New York City, around 8 P.M. and took the subway directly to the Lower Manhattan church whose staff had asked for our help.

By that time, we had been traveling, due to delays, for seventeen hours.

While waiting for the subway, I told the team members with me, "I hope your expectation isn't to go to bed, because that's not been my experience during disasters. I fully expect we will be up all night working, beginning as soon as we get there." And that is exactly what happened.

As we walked in the church's door, we were greeted by a woman named Leah, a law-school student who had taken a leave of absence the day after the attack to coordinate relief-effort volunteer services through the church. She, like so many New Yorkers we would meet, had never done trauma or disaster work yet would do a marvelous job in the face of this challenge.

"Are you the guys from California?" were her first words to us.

"We are," one of my team members said.

"Do you want to go talk to firefighters?"

"Yes, great," I replied, expecting to head straight to the ground zero area.

"They're on Staten Island."

Staten Island, a borough of New York City, is about thirty minutes by ferryboat from Manhattan. And we weren't even going by boat. "We're going to throw you in a van," she explained, "and it's probably going to take an hour and a half to two hours to drive you over there with all the barricades."

Staten Island? I was thinking. *Here we are, all the way from California, standing in Manhattan so close to ground zero we can smell the smoke, and now we're going to go two hours by car away from the whole thing?*

We went, of course.

And our experience there would turn out to be the next surprise—in fact, the very foundation of all that was to follow.

Chapter **Two**

Homeport

September 18, 2001

After navigating the streets of Lower Manhattan, around and through barricades and checkpoints, closed streets and guarded bridges, our van finally connected with the expressways leading to Staten Island. A few minutes later, we arrived at an area that looked very much like a military complex. Military police were standing sentry at the gate. At the time, I didn't know whether the military presence was because of the World Trade Center attack or whether we were arriving at a military base. I found out we were entering the Homeport Naval Station on Staten Island, a decommissioned naval station that was being used as the staging area and recovery station for all the Staten Island–based firefighters and rescue personnel working at ground zero.

We stepped into a room the size of an armory, and into a typhoon of activity. On one side stood medical infirmary units with nurses and doctors, on the other, an entire information setup, complete with computer laptops, wired and ready. Over here were big-screen televisions, over there, cots and sleeping materials. From my left came the *beep-beep-beep* of loaded trucks moving in reverse; from the right, a voice called, "Hey, we need help over here," and a dozen volunteers rushed by us to unpack the truck. Everywhere, it seemed, were long tables filled with a warehouse of stuff—cereals, milk, food, underwear, sweaters, masks, helmets, protein bars, candy, water, Chap Stick—anything anybody could ever need. And amid it all were hundreds of firefighters, police officers, and volunteers waiting to work.

"Are you the chaplains?" a female voice called to us.

"Yes," we responded to a woman rushing toward us.

"Oh! Oh, I can't believe it!" she exclaimed and grabbed me by my arm. Her name was Ronnie. "Go-getter" didn't begin to describe this dynamo. She was the kind of woman who'd seen pretty much everything, the kind who just gets better, stronger. And her heart was as bold as her Staten Island accent. People were vying for her attention, yet she kept putting them off, her grip still firmly on my arm. I was going nowhere. "Hold on just a second," she would say over her shoulder. "I need to talk to these guys right now!"

"Are you the Red Cross?" I asked, somewhat bewildered at the magnitude of the energy bursting from this place.

"No, no, no," she said with a flip of a wrist.

"Are you the Salvation Army?"

"No, no, none of those," she said.

Those were the two organizations I was used to seeing at disasters. But this was something different altogether, a can-do volunteer attitude I would see often during the weeks ahead. Ronnie and the rest of Staten Island's residents had an eyewitness vantage point for the attack so close to home that it must have felt like it was happening in their front yards. So she and her community volunteer friends—not the armed services, not the Red Cross, not the Salvation Army, not the government, just good-hearted, strong-minded Staten Island citizens—immediately went into action.

Every year this group coordinates a "fleet week" when navy ships sail into town, a wonderful event that celebrates the U.S. Navy's history on their island in all sorts of fun ways. They considered this "their" Homeport, and they knew the station's community day room was totally equipped for such a situation. It had full-blown showers, a full-blown kitchen, a full-blown storage warehouse, and an enormous area able to handle almost everything else. So, with the aid and support of Homeport's authorities, along with the donations from the island's businesses and churches, they created a place to meet the physical needs of the tidal wave of relief workers coming and going to the disaster site from here. The Coast Guard, I was told, had lent their chaplains for the workers during the first week, but they had moved on to other assignments. So by the night I arrived, Homeport had everything to meet the workers' needs—that is, almost everything, as Ronnie explained while still holding on to my forearm.

"I've got a telephone, I've got computers, I've got food, I've got resources, I've got money, I've got all these things. But you know what I don't have? I don't have God in the house," she said, and then she let go of my arm and stood back, as if to say, *Well, get to work.*

At that moment I realized the irony of our standing there at all. We had flown cross-country prepared to deal with whatever official channels were in effect in order to gain access to the firefighters and other workers. But now we had been brought to a place, almost instantly, where the rescue workers would be brought to us, shift after shift. Wisely, Ronnie and the Homeport authorities had grasped the relief workers' special need for chaplains. Their mission of mercy was to provide relief for these rescue workers who were themselves survivors. That was one of the unique aspects of this disaster. Homeport was a staging area for firefighters and other rescue personnel on their way to work. Yet, at the same time, it was also their relief center, because most of the workers were either survivors or victims of the crisis they were working, having all lost brothers, colleagues, or friends in the attack.

Near us, a large group of firefighters were in one area, waiting anxiously for the call to head to ground zero. We could feel the tension, the energy, across the entire station as we sat down with the firefighters and began to talk.

We introduced ourselves to a few of them, trying our best not to trample into their privacy too clumsily. Soon I asked about Ray Downey, the leader of the New York Fire Department's elite USAR squad I'd met in Oklahoma. The NY-USAR squad had dealt with both the 1993 World Trade Center bombing and the 1995 Oklahoma City disaster, back when blown-up buildings in America was still a novelty. During our work at Oklahoma City, we had volunteered to serve on the overnight shift so the local clergy could rest and be ready to work with the traumatized citizens in their parishes, synagogues, and congregations during the day. Some of the USAR teams had chaplains, but New York City's team did not. I had been born and spent part of my early childhood in the New York area, so I naturally gravitated to this expert group. For the next four to five days, when they showed up for work at the Oklahoma City bombing site, I worked with them. When they ate, I ate; when they went in the building's ruins, I went in the building's ruins. When they needed water, I got them water. When they needed to laugh, we laughed; when they needed to cry, we cried. And when they needed to talk, we talked. We became close in the way only people in such situations do.

As soon as I asked the Staten Island firefighters what happened to Downey's team, the firefighters began to open up.

"Big losses with those guys. They were in there," one of the men said. "Downey was one of them." In the first moments of the crisis, the fire department's senior leadership had rushed to set up a command center at the base of the towers, and many had been lost in the collapse of the buildings. The fact that we had worked with Downey and his team and now were mourning them was all these men needed.

"Come on, Chaplain," one said. "You be with us tonight."

And so that night they told us their stories. They knew we would understand. We would not be shocked at the graphic nature of the images they were carrying around with them.

"I was running toward the towers after the first plane hit

when everyone thought it had been only an accident," one said. "Suddenly, I hear another plane, far too low and far too fast. I could hear the roar of the engines. I look up to see the second plane pass overhead, then I hear a huge explosion. The second tower had just been hit."

"I had just arrived, in full gear," said another. "I could see other firefighters and their fire engine ahead of me. Then the building started falling down, and we were all running for our lives. The cloud was barreling down the street on top of us, and we were all diving under cars, diving through windows to get out of the suffocating ash cloud's path."

Another said, "I was in the south tower as it began to collapse. I remember feeling the brush of the explosion, being driven into a wall and then underneath a fire engine. I don't even know how I'm alive."

Another fully outfitted firefighter had been heading toward the towers, part of the next wave of firefighters to go in. "We could feel the heat a block away as we were going forward. You could see the stuff falling from the sky onto the people on the street. And I'm thinking we better take shelter; we better get out of the way. A third plane could be coming."

"What did you do?" I asked.

"We kept going forward," he answered. "Then they held us back. It was pure chaos. Our squad chiefs were trying to figure out who was doing what, waiting for orders of some kind. What we didn't know was that the first command center had been demolished by that time, and we were having to wait for a second command center to be established. So we're waiting, we're watching, and then we hear a rumble and a shudder from the first building as it collapsed."

I'll never forget how he paused, his voice dropping to a murmur. "Chaplain, had those towers fallen an hour later, we'd have lost a thousand firefighters—because we would have all been in the building."

According to a *USA Today* in-depth report published two months after the attack, 479 rescue professionals died during the evacuation that day. Of those, 23 were cops, and 113 were port authority officers, officials, and security guards. Three were women: a port authority captain, a police officer, and a paramedic. The rest were firefighters, 343 dying in the line of duty. The New York Fire Department had been founded in 1865. In all the years preceding September 11, 2001, it had lost only 778 firefighters in the line of duty.

Purportedly, an accurate headcount was impossible for days after the attack because no one knew exactly who had answered the call. Many firefighters had jumped on fire trucks instead of going home at the shift change. Other firefighters who had been visiting firehouses across the city when the call came in, ones on medical leave or recently retired, had also joined in. By all accounts, every firefighter in the entire city had sprinted toward the site. One group purportedly commandeered a crowded city bus and headed it toward the flames. During the earliest hours of the disaster, entire companies went unaccounted for, no one knowing whether they were buried under the collapsed towers or simply too busy to check in. A *Washington Post* reporter called it an "heroic act of insubordination." So many commanders died in the collapse that Mayor Rudolph Giuliani promoted more than 160 new officers to fill the leadership void. Every firehouse, every squad was affected in some way. For example, eleven firefighters from Rescue 1 ran toward the towers. None came back. I quickly came to understand the saying, "All gave some, some gave all."

Throughout the night, the Homeport firefighters told their stories. They talked of their boots melting, their ears bleeding, their hats smoking, their eyes swelling shut from the smoke and dust. They talked of the struggle to find survivors in the immediate rubble, the horror of reaching for a hand and finding nothing more, the dodging of shooting flames and deadly debris. I began to hear common threads of anguish. The hardest part of the experience, most would say, was just the Why? "Why did God allow this to happen?" many pointedly asked.

But perhaps even more pervasive was the guilt. Survivor's guilt was a stunning reality for these firefighters. Most I encountered were grappling hard with it.

"I was so helpless," one said. "I was standing right there when it all collapsed, but I couldn't save anybody!"

Another said, "Why did I run away when I should have run toward it?"

Yet if they hadn't run, they would have been killed. That unalterable fact was common knowledge. They *had* to run *away* from the problem, all the while knowing they'd been trained to run *toward* the problem. There was a big difference between choosing to move ahead, knowing death was possible or even likely—and moving ahead, knowing death was definite, without any possibility of saving lives in the sacrifice. That distinction, however, did little to assuage the pain I heard. The guilt of having to choose survival over duty must have been almost too much to bear.

Beyond the guilt, however, there was an even more common emotion. They all shared a sheer, white-hot rage.

One firefighter found the words to express it: "I just have all this anger. I didn't realize I was capable of rage. It is not going away, and now I just want to hit something; I want to hurt somebody. I just want to grab something and smash it."

At that time I had only seen what the television cameras had shown of the event, a horrific sight but still a step removed from the reality of the World Trade Center ruins only a few miles away. Soon I would understand all too well.

WE TALKED WITH THE RESCUE WORKERS at Homeport all night and into the next day, only taking a break to take care of our gear.

Then, about 1 P.M., someone yelled, "Let's go."

The firemen around us jumped up and headed for the door.

"You going with us?" several of the firefighters called back.

It took me a moment to realize that the firefighters were going to ground zero, and they were inviting us along. Surely there were official channels to go through to gain the badges needed inside the fenced-off areas. Could we just get up and go with them?

But there was another question beyond whether we could go. *Should* we go? After being so close to ground zero and almost instantly being led here instead, somehow this now seemed right. I hadn't cared if we ever got to ground zero. Maybe this was where we were supposed to be. This hometown relief center was legit, and there was a community streaming through here that needed what we came to offer. The work we could do here could easily be enough reason to justify the trip from California. That I knew from experience. But my experience also told me something else. Another aspect of the checks and balances we used to make sure our focus stayed off ourselves and on those who needed our help was that we had to be ready for anything God had in mind. That "rule" had taught us to be open to constant surprise. And, I had to admit, this was yet another surprise.

"You going?" yet another fireman called back.

"You think the commander will okay it?" I asked.

Within seconds, I was standing in front of the battalion commander, who was assigning firefighters to the three buses awaiting transport.

"Got room for the chaplain, sir?" the firefighter asked.

His answer was to put us right on the buses with the group surrounding us.

Just before the buses left, the battalion commander asked me, "Chaplain, would you say a prayer before we go?" It then occurred to me that these men were grieving, not only for their comrades and their leadership heroes, but for one of their spiritual heroes as well, a beloved senior fire chaplain, Father Mychal Judge, who had died during the first minutes of the disaster. I knew the story, already legendary, about the death of the beloved senior New York Fire Department chaplain, the crisis event's first official death, his death certificate bearing the number 00001.

The story, described by one journalist later as the first "poetry" of the disaster, had begun to circulate during the earliest hours. "Father Mike," as all his firefighters called him, was believed to have been killed by falling debris while saying last rites over a firefighter killed by a victim who had fallen from one of the highest floors. The truth, which came later, seemed no less compelling. After being seen kneeling to give the last rites to the dead firefighter, another fire official had seen him a few moments later inside the lobby of Tower One, the north tower, where he must have rushed farther into the danger just before the south tower's collapse. That's where he was found dead from the force of the first tower's explosion.

One of the most searing images of the tragedy was of a group of dust-covered firemen and rescue officials carrying his body to the sidewalk near a command post only minutes before the north tower collapsed. The firefighters had gently laid his blue fire jacket over his face then rushed back into the danger. From there, his body somehow found its way to the altar of nearby St. Peter's Catholic Church, his badge and helmet resting on his chest. He became Victim #1 and, for the entire city's fire service, a near-sacred symbol of this new century's day of infamy.

"Chief," I said, "I would consider it an honor."

Chapter Three

Ground Zero

September 19, 2001

. . . I am at ground zero. Pray Hard.

THE RIDE BACK TO GROUND ZERO on the fire squads' buses
was dramatically different from the van ride we had taken only
hours before, in reverse. Now we were riding with a police escort
and using special reserved emergency-vehicle lanes. What had
taken us almost two hours the night before now required only
thirty minutes. Soon we were driving through Lower Manhattan
again. And as we rode, I was struck by the firefighters' faces—
their determination and yet their exhaustion, fatigue battling
fierce commitment.

A rainstorm had just ended. What should have smelled fresh
was acrid; what should have looked clean was damp and ashen.
Our bus approached the area surrounding the sixteen-acre World
Trade Center disaster site that comprised the WTC complex. It
had been cordoned off with a temporary wall made of police
barricades and chain-link fencing. Our special buses were allowed
into the heart of the ground zero area of the terrorist attack, but

not without an official escort. We went through checkpoint after checkpoint manned by military police. I had seen this sort of setup in Oklahoma City with its marshal law feel, but nothing to this extent. The enormity of it all was overwhelming. Even the buses full of firefighters were being checked for badges. I expected to need a badge, but the size of this event obviously demanded much more security than one measly badge; everyone I saw was wearing a handful. A guardsman asked for mine. "He's with me," the battalion chief said.

"No problem, Chaplain," the National Guardsman responded.

Finally, three blocks from ground zero, the buses stopped. We deployed and saw where we were headed. There, before us, loomed the collapsed remains of two of the country's tallest buildings, a pile of debris more than twenty stories high in some places. The debris looked like an enormous broken pile of steel-beam Tinkertoys, a hovering mass of rubble. The collapsed pile filled the entire interior area of the ruined buildings; all four corners of the street blocks that had surrounded the World Trade Center towers were literally filled with this massive pile of bent and twisted steel and rubble. The rubble even pressed beyond the buildings' boundaries, damaging neighboring structures drastically and dramatically.

As we moved closer, my senses were on overload. The noise, the smell, the destruction—my mind went reeling back to Oklahoma City. I was at the Murrah Federal Building again and in autopilot mode, except this was the equivalent of a thousand Oklahoma Citys. Windows all around us were broken out.

Electrical conduits, venetian blinds, broken glass, and building beams were all exposed. Street signs were destroyed. Corners of buildings were smashed, and awnings were ripped off as if a hurricane had blown through each alleyway. We continued heading north, still circling the pile. The buildings, the trees, the streets were covered with soot and dust. The trees were blanketed with ash and paper particles so deep the scene resembled a dirty New York snowfall. Paper litter from the millions of sheets of paper from the thousands of destroyed offices was everywhere. I could make out the writing on a couple of pages at my feet. One was someone's payroll information; another was someone's loan documents. What we saw most was a vast amount of twisted, bent aluminum siding sheets and metal girders. No personal items, no furniture, no computers. Where was it all?

The ruins were still on fire; smoke was billowing from everywhere, giving what was already ominous an even more hellish quality. It felt like we were going into battle. The air was filled with the smell of fire, concrete particles, and melting steel. Even now, writing about it, I can still smell it—a dusty, sweet, wet, caustic odor. I was later told that the tons of concrete had landed so hard they had been pulverized. The cement was now part of the air.

"How many bombs hit this place?" I gasped.

Television didn't capture the reality. Having spent part of my childhood in Europe only a generation after World War II, I had been surrounded with the living memory of the war's destruction. And what I was seeing now conjured up old images of villages leveled by sustained bombardment by artillery shells.

Except for the pile. Nothing I had ever seen compared to the sky-high pile of debris from the collapsed towers' crumbled remains. Before us, above us, we could see the rescue workers, at least two thousand people working across the surface. Outfitted in vinyl slickers because of the rain, they were yellow blurs of color scattered across what we could see of the top of the debris. Teams from across the country and around the world were there. Mexico's urban search and rescue squad was one of many I recognized. "Rat people," their USAR team members were called, those who specialized in going under buildings leveled by earthquakes. There were many, many dog rescue teams. My eyes immediately landed on a team that included a golden retriever and a Jack Russell terrier, exactly like my own dogs at home. I tried not to think about the ones who had died in the first hours of the wreckage while trying to save trapped humans.

The firefighters were working with only flashlights and shovels, while the special urban search and rescue squads worked from their own command areas using sophisticated listening equipment and camera devices to probe into the pile's pockets. Everything seemed to be happening at once. It was a bizarre, amazing sight.

I had once read the specifics of these towers. It had taken ten years to build them. Construction had required excavation to bedrock seventy feet down, and the reclaimed material had been used as landfill to create Battery Park City, a 23.5-acre urban renewal project that revitalized Lower Manhattan, now evacuated and endangered by flooding from the surrounding Hudson River.

The buildings had weighed more than 1.5 million tons. They had contained 198 miles of heating ducts, 23,000 fluorescent light bulbs, 10 million square feet of space, 43,600 windows, and 194 passenger elevators. Now it all lay in one colossal heap before me.

Eerily, the pile itself seemed a presence. Oklahoma City's site was a bombed nine-story building that remained standing throughout the rescue work. In Oklahoma, the smell was diesel fuel from the fertilizer-based bomb, and the soot was black. But comparisons were a wasted effort. The remains of two 110-story buildings were resting before us, and the adjacent buildings still standing were 40-story structures, now gaping and ripped. My eyes caught on twig-like structures sticking out of several of the ruined buildings. The sight was hard to comprehend by the human eye—twenty-ton beams falling from the Twin Towers had sliced through these buildings, splitting them wide open.

And everywhere was the smoke and the heat. The fire underneath the pile was sixteen hundred degrees Fahrenheit. The beams being removed from inside were still red hot; the firefighters had to hose down the metal. The concrete dust had trapped in the radiation.

And, most eerily, the pile was *moving* . . . As heavy equipment crept over it, the whole immense mass quivered under our feet.

The firefighters at Homeport had vividly described their rage. Now I understood. This moving mass of steel, the fire rising from below the girders, the clouds of green-and-yellow smoke, the heat and the intensity and the sheer enormity of it—this was the very face of evil. At that instant, and for many of the nights to come, I wanted to scream at this thing. This was as close to hell as I ever wanted to be.

As the day went on, I would keep seeing the scorch behind my eyelids when I closed my eyes . . . *every* time I closed my eyes. *No,* I kept telling myself. *That is not the picture I want to leave with, the picture I'll see in my dreams. I do not want to leave a victim of this.* I knew I would be of no use if I did not fight that image. The only way to help the rescue workers as they dug for others trapped in the pile, I quickly realized, was to help keep their minds above while their hands were below. So I had to find a way *not* to dwell on what was underneath the rubble. I had to keep my own focus above, or I would be no help at all.

I had brought my Palm Pilot. I opened it and tapped out a message, the first and the shortest of many journal entries I would send back home:

I am at ground zero. Pray Hard.

WE STOPPED NEAR THE PILE by the interior perimeter and waited for direction. Our lieutenants and captains returned to us after discussing with their commanders how best to divide our 180 firefighters. Four command centers had been established around the edges of the site. The group nearest me was told to go to the command post on Vesey Street. I nodded to my chaplaincy team member who would be going with firefighters in the opposite direction. We'd stay in touch by cell phone. My group began to move. We were facing north, and at that time, buses couldn't get to the west side of the cordoned-off area because there was no street. It was buried under ruins, the debris having been blown all the way to where we stood. Only a walkway had been cut through it. But the confusion was enormous. Just getting your bearings was problematic, even for the firemen and other rescue personnel familiar with the area before the attack. One exasperated firefighter explained how it had been one of the biggest problems since the first day: "They'd tell us to go to Tower One, stairwell three. We'd just look at each other. First, who knew where Tower One was anymore, and how do you even begin to locate stairwell three?"

On foot, we began to circle the ground zero area, walking through the cleared sections. As we moved through the interior, I found myself looking up with almost every step. We could hear glass falling from the damaged buildings we were passing, each crash reminding us what was morbidly apparent: We were in a very dangerous place. I noticed a large fluorescent X on each building we passed. Above or below each X was scrawled "Engine 17" or "Ladder 117," or a different unit number—the all-clear markings of the firefighter crews who had risked their lives to look for survivors inside each building. The last time I had seen that kind of mark was Oklahoma City, where dozens of damaged buildings eventually showed the A-OK scrawl.

Finally, we arrived at the Vesey Street command station, a group of wooden huts. Inside were drafting boards holding site plans and commanders manning hand-held radios. We were encircled now by twisted aluminum skirting—the buildings' "skin," the workers called it—along with fragmented fiber and mounds of dirt from the tunneling.

But what surprised me most were the hundreds and hundreds of firefighters lining the primitive paths cleared around the command center. Most were sitting on overturned plastic buckets, no doubt the same pails used by the bucket brigades we had seen on television during the first hours of the rescue attempt as people moved the rubble hand to hand in hopes of rescuing buried survivors. We were part of a shift change, so deployments from other areas of the city were arriving as well, yet everyone was just sitting. Meanwhile, from beyond the mass of firefighters came the din of heavy machinery being moved into the area and of fully loaded dump trucks roaring out. Big flatbed trucks carrying huge excavators were passing by. And down the roadway, cranes extending over a block in length were being assembled.

Someone told me what was happening. Heavy equipment was now being moved in to speed up the removal of the crushed girders. Therefore only a certain number of firefighter squads at a time were being allowed to go onto the pile to work by hand. All the firefighters stretching down the road were being forced to wait their turn to work. And their frustration was palpable. Most still believed that if they were allowed to keep digging by hand they could still find their comrades alive. We were not twenty-five yards from ground zero at this point; we could see the fires burning, see people working. Yet the firefighters were forced to sit and watch. Squad after squad were sitting, waiting around the perimeter of the work site to get the order to go onto the beams.

And as we all waited, we were specifically ordered to stand off the pile. I noticed a certain obvious reverence everyone had for the pile—not the reverence for a holy thing but an evil one. There was a respect for its danger, a respect that this thing had taken lives. Even to stand on the edge of the pile was putting yourself in danger, especially with the heavy equipment moving by us, up and into it.

I scanned the thousands of yellow-clad workers already inside working on the pile. I was surprised at the noticeable absence of clergy at the site. I saw only one other chaplain, a priest in full fire service gear including a helmet reading "fire chaplain"; he had a younger man wearing a clergy collar in tow. I watched how, as they moved from one spot to another, the rescue workers gravitated toward them, trying to make eye contact and receiving what seemed to be spoken blessings such as "Blessings on you; be safe," and other words of comfort. From what I could see, those two clergy members were the only ones on the site during that shift, at least until we had arrived with the firefighters.

"Going forward" into a disaster site, as I called it, was not common for most chaplains in the first place. I had become comfortable fulfilling that role in Oklahoma City, as well as during other disaster relief efforts, but I knew I wasn't the only one, and I was surprised not to see more of the clergy inside the perimeter. Since this was a very big disaster, I figured that others must be out of my sight. Later, when I had a chance to talk to the younger priest, I learned that because the interior site itself was so chaotic and so many well-meaning but untrained clergy had appeared, access had been denied to almost all but the obviously attired priests and chaplains until some protocol was established.

Our plans had been to stick with those who had brought us, to adopt them, much as we'd done with Ray Downey and the New York USAR team in Oklahoma City. But that's not the way the scene unfolded. The rescue squads were being created as they arrived, so almost immediately, the men on our buses were scattered across the site, and us with them. Since we were not going to be able to adopt a certain crew, we were going to adopt whoever came our way, whoever needed what we were there to give. So as they sat, waiting, we chose a group to sit with—or more often, they chose us.

We were sitting on makeshift chairs and benches and buckets, whatever we could find. Thirty minutes went by, then an hour, two, four, six, then eight hours, as the squad lieutenants continued to check, to pace, and then to wait some more to take their men into work.

Of our twelve-hour shift that night, ten hours would be spent waiting, first at the Vesey command center and then at the West Highway center. We had lots of time to think as we breathed the foul air we knew had to be toxic. And through it all, we continued to talk to the hundreds of men waiting in both areas.

Actually, the forced waiting was good in one important way. The squad members couldn't work, but they could talk. They had a chance to tell their stories, or cry, or pray with somebody. The baby faces broke my heart—these twenty-three-, twenty-four-, twenty-five-year-old firefighters and police officers, and the National Guard men and women who were even younger, some only nineteen or twenty years old. They were so young to be looking at such horror. I couldn't help but wonder about the lasting impact this experience would have on their lives. I knew that a large number of the workers who responded to the Oklahoma City disaster had retired from their fire service or search and rescue squads as a result of the horror they saw.

In the days ahead, I would talk to many young relief workers—guardsmen, paramedics, search and rescue experts, and police officers as well as firefighters. So many of them would feel like the twenty-year-old Air National Guard member and would, as she did, fight hard to hide their fears. When I asked her how she was doing, she couldn't answer for a moment; the words wouldn't come. She believed in God, she said, but her faith was shaken badly after what she'd seen since being at ground zero. She couldn't put into words everything she was feeling, and she couldn't get what she was seeing out of her head.

"It's all so much," she admitted as we talked. "I'm afraid I won't be able to get rid of what's in my mind."

As other Air Guardsmen came our way, I gave her a quick hug and a whispered "God bless you," so I wouldn't embarrass her in front of them.

Even the most experienced firefighters were having trouble expressing what they'd seen, though. I recall hearing a fellow chaplain put the situation well: For the victims' families, it was horrible not to know; for these men, it was horrible *to* know. One seasoned firefighter I met that night, a veteran of many fires, many rescues, and many fatalities, could hardly talk without breaking down.

After the first few hours, I realized that these men had not told anyone the things they were expressing to us. In the nine days since the attack, most of them had been living on autopilot fueled by pure adrenaline to do what they had to do. Most of them had not taken time to tell their stories to someone, and I knew from long experience that the first step in coping with a trauma is to talk about it.

So I began to ask questions that would allow them to tell their stories but would also allow me to assess their needs. As each talked, I would have the opportunity to listen, which is the very heart of all we do—studied, dedicated listening to people in crisis. Doing so not only showed we cared but also gave those sharing their stories permission to begin to process, to handle what was happening to them.

Two simple questions became the foundation of every encounter after that, for me and for all our team chaplains in the weeks ahead:

The first question: "Where were you when the attack occurred?"

The second: "What is the hardest part for you?"

One firefighter's anguished answers seemed symbolic of all the stories that night. He'd been in the fire service nineteen years, as had a buddy he'd known since childhood. His lifelong friend was one of the firefighters trapped in the collapse. "You want to know what the hardest part is?" he repeated, fidgeting with his pickax, twirling it around and around and around. "He's in there, and I can't get in there to find him." As we talked, the rain had begun to fall again, and I don't think he even noticed, being so fixated on the pile and his friend lying somewhere inside it. He'd get up, walk around, and disappear. Each time, I'd wonder if he had pushed his way into the pile against orders. But he always returned, twirling his pickax and fidgeting without ceasing.

Finally I asked one of the other squad members, "Is he okay?"

The firefighter's answer was sheer truth. "As okay as the rest of us," he said.

As we waited and waited, the stories filled the time and space around us just as they had at Homeport. Many firefighters talked about what it was like to go "underneath." While the whole area seemed pancaked from top to bottom, it wasn't quite true, and that fueled hopes for survivors. The rescue work centered around pockets of space that were everywhere in the ruins—"voids," the workers called them—between fallen girders and the rubble, especially stairwells where people could be trapped alive. But excavation was also happening around the edges and below. Early on, firefighters had been able to get to the underground floors of the World Trade Center. They told me of the eerie scenes of flooding around the towers' foundations, of massive beams and concrete pieces driven like projectiles into the subway areas, of underground shops and mall areas that were perfectly intact.

One firefighter explained the sixth sense many rescue workers develop. He had descended into the flooded areas of the buildings' lowest underground levels immediately after the collapse. "I went in places beyond my personal safety zone down there," he said.

"Safety zone?" I asked.

"Yeah, where you know you're at your edge, and if you go any farther, you're going to be across the line. Pushing fate, you know? There were a few times where I knew I was pushing too far." He had ventured into voids only big enough to allow him to shimmy through to bigger voids. Then he'd do it again, moving deeper into yet another pocket, as if he were in a cave created by twisted-steel pickup sticks. He knew that the slightest change in the pile could trap him, and he knew each extra second could be a second too long, a step too far. Yet he had done it anyway. "It was the first time I've ever consciously put myself in a situation where I knew I was beyond peril," he admitted.

"Why did you do it?" I asked.

"We were sure we were going to find somebody," he answered. "That's the reason we kept going."

The last survivor had been rescued less than forty-eight hours after the attack. No one had been found alive since, and we were at Day Nine. They had uncovered remains but no one alive. For rescue workers, ground-level fatalities were understood, manageable, just a part of their job. Even the gruesome reality, for instance, of filling buckets with fingers found in the first hours— the only remains of many caught in the explosion, their bodies shattered so completely—the rescue workers were able to accept. But they could do so because they believed they were still going to rescue survivors caught in those voids, waiting to be freed.

It had been raining off and on for several days. And it would rain again that night as well as the next night—Day Ten. That would be a night of miserable, cold, driving, dangerous rain that would whip through the interior of ground zero, tornado-like, blowing loose material off nearby roofs. But I recall being momentarily hopeful as it drenched us all.

A firefighter standing near me cursed the rain.

When I said I was actually thankful for the wet weather, he shot me something beyond a puzzled look. "Thankful? How come?"

"Because it might be the only chance we have for finding anyone alive," I answered. The human body can go forty days without food but only about ten days without water because of dehydration. And we were pushing that deadline hard. I thought of the 1989 Loma Peralta earthquake in the San Francisco Bay area, one of our first major recovery effort experiences. On October 17, at 5:04 P.M., 67 people died and 3,757 were injured in the massive fifteen-second earthquake. Rescuers worked for days, digging and looking for survivors on a pancaked freeway in Oakland. The search went on, car by car, most flattened by a fallen overpass. Only the rain from the October bay area weather offered hope that those trapped could still be living as the days passed. And that was exactly what had happened for the last survivor rescued, a man found days later on the floorboard of his crushed truck. The rain had kept him alive.

Hope is a hard thing to let die. And while I waited with the New York City firefighters for a chance to rescue someone, anyone, we let it fuel us just as it had in San Francisco, against all odds, against the truth.

FINALLY, THE CALL CAME. Each squad's lieutenants delivered the news: We were going in. A rush of adrenaline, a quick prayer, and we were finally on the move.

During the endless hours of waiting, I had realized that I was about to become not only a chaplain but a rescue worker as well. Every pair of hands was crucial as the clock was ticking on that hydration deadline, but I also knew that was how I and my team members worked best. The work of a crisis chaplain takes many forms. As mentioned earlier, our greatest experience in past disasters had been in a side-by-side presence, "going forward" into the pile, either working alongside or just being there alongside those who worked. During our years of crisis intervention we had been trained to perform the traditional roles played by chaplains and other clergy members as well as those performed by the Salvation Army and the Red Cross—working off-site with rescue workers, survivors, and victims' families in need of counseling. Over the years, though, we had adopted a more proactive approach. We always submitted to the authority of the day, just as we had done at Homeport. If the firefighters had not invited us along, we would have worked with the rescue workers on their return, but we always preferred to go forward "into the event" with rescue workers versus staying back.

So I approached a lieutenant of one of the squads with whom I had spent the last ten hours. I had waited when they waited, now I would dig when they dug. "That okay, lieutenant?"

"You sure about that, chaplain?"

"Yes sir."

"Then you're with us. Let's go."

We walked through an entranceway cut into the pile. We went deep into the middle, basically climbing up, slowly, across the beams. We had to be very careful about how we stepped. The pile moved constantly, shaking, rumbling as the construction equipment passed. There were voids underneath our feet; this was not solid ground.

As we inched down the twisted hillside, over new sections exposed by the constant cutting, hoisting, and carrying away of beam after beam, we were told to look for any signs of life—or death.

My squad was assigned a certain area of newly exposed voids. One worker would go in each hole, search it with a flashlight, and then, when nothing was found, we'd all move to the next one, where another of us would climb over the steamy rubble to peer inside. As the heavy equipment was cutting and removing rebar, the reinforcing steel inside concrete, we inched along, working by hand, the beams flattened by the impact hanging precariously over us. The temperature on the pile was close to 110 degrees. On the sidewalk or on the street below, it was 70 degrees, yet on the pile it hovered beyond the century mark. We began to sweat so much we all wanted to take off our heavy gear. We especially wanted to take off our gloves, the heat was so bad, but wires were exposed everywhere we looked. A fellow worker's slightest step could send debris flying. So much was reported about glass shards cutting the rescue dogs' feet that the Humane Society was inundated with donated dog booties.

As equipment operators cut through beams, tied them off, lifted them up, and moved them away, we continued checking pockets, listening for any sound and sniffing for any odor. Sometimes we worked as if we were on an archeological dig, using shovels and picks, looking closely at everything that was uncovered.

A nearby squad was working in an area near a train station stairwell when one of the firefighters thought he saw movement. He called out. Everyone rushed to the area. Lights were moved and turned on full blast. "Stokes basket" stretchers were brought over. Sophisticated camera equipment was readied, and a dog rescue team was brought in. In the days since the attack, dogs had been asked to do many tasks such as being dropped by basket into search areas and sent underground wearing cameras. Now the trainer sent one of his dogs into the tunnel. It was an eerie moment as the dog disappeared, and we all stared after him into the dark.

Two minutes passed. Then three. Someone whispered, "Where's the dog? Where's the dog!"

Our unspoken hope, the anticipation, was that the dog might

appear, leading somebody out. I was praying, *Lord, just give us one person from this thing.* I wasn't bargaining with God for thousands, even though thousands were missing. I was praying for just one . . . to make it all worthwhile today.

But then the dog returned. Alone.

The extra lights were turned off, the Stokes baskets were carried off, and several hundred people walked away in absolute silence.

Later, as I was working near one of the Tower One stairwell fragments, I began talking to one of the workers who was visibly upset. Unable to hold it in any longer, he was sitting with his head in his hands.

"This is hard," I said.

"Yeah," he murmured, as if he were talking to himself. "But the worst part is that they survived, and we aren't going to get to them in time."

Gradually the dawning horror of such knowledge hit me. They *knew.* Of course. The firefighters obviously had been in radio contact with some of the trapped people, and the medical examiners could tell from the retrieved bodies how and when they had died.

One encounter, during the late-night work in the days ahead, brought that grim reality home. I had noticed an older man who looked like a retired firefighter talking to the young firefighters, one on one, for long periods of time, almost as if he were coaching them. When, inevitably, each young man would begin to cry, the older man would put a hand behind the firefighter's head, pull the young man into his chest, and hug him. He was loving them through the most difficult time of their young careers. I was proud of him, of his deep love for these men and the love and respect they were showing for him. After about an hour or so, as I was getting ready to move, I decided to thank him for his work. As I approached him, though, his eyes welled up with tears. I embraced him. "Thank you," I said. "God has to be proud of your service to these young men tonight. Were you a firefighter?"

And that's when I found out the tragic extent of the service he had truly given.

"Yes," he said. "But that's not why I'm here. My sons are here."

At first I thought he meant they were working on the pile, much as we were. But he was pointing.

Down.

The man had two sons—one was a firefighter, the other a police officer. And somehow he knew where they both were. One son was in the north tower when it collapsed. "He is somewhere down there," the father explained. "And my other son is still somewhere over there." He pointed toward the south tower area.

I couldn't speak; I could only hug him again as we parted. But inside I was weeping at the thought of this man's sacrifice. I thought of fathers and sons, of my own son, Kyle, and how much I loved him. And all I could do was silently pray that God the Father would be able to offer this father some peace.

The next night I saw him back again on the pile. With him was a young police officer. The officer told me that the police department had assigned him to transport this father to and from the scene. The retired firefighter had come every day since the attack for ten hours a day to encourage other fathers' sons as he waited for his own sons to be recovered.

WE FOUND NOTHING THAT NIGHT, no one. Dead or alive. It would be the same story for days. The futility was taking its toll. As one of the multiple-ton cranes was being repositioned, a dozen of us took a break. One of my chaplain team members, a man named Ryan, was standing beside a firefighter who had a faraway, detached look. I heard Ryan ask him how he was coping. Barely changing expression, the firefighter mentioned he had lost forty friends on September 11. Not colleagues, not acquaintances—friends.

"Your family must have been so happy to see you," Ryan responded.

A cloud passed over the firefighter's face. He had gone home to a big celebration, he answered, complete with a homemade banner created by his family. It had said in big red letters: "We are proud of you, Dad. You're our hero!" But he hadn't been able to handle it; he hadn't even let his wife hug him.

Ryan frowned. "Why?"

"I don't feel like a hero," he mumbled. "I didn't die."

Ryan shook his head. "But don't you see? We know you *would* have died—that you would have sacrificed yourself just as your friends did. That's why your family, all of us, know in our minds and hearts what you would have done for us."

That seemed to stir something in the firefighter; the faraway look vanished.

"Have you talked to your kids about this?" Ryan coaxed.

He shrugged. "My son keeps asking, but I can't talk about it. I just have to leave the room," the firefighter answered, chin out. "I have to be strong for him."

"But you have to talk to him."

"I can't—I have to be strong for him."

"What does being strong have to do with not talking to him?" Ryan finally asked.

"If I talk about it, I'll break down," he admitted. "And I've *got* to be strong in front of him. I can't let him see me cry."

"Who in the world told you that?"

The firefighter stared at the chaplain. "Are you saying . . . that it's okay for him to see me cry?"

"It's not just okay, it's essential. He *needs* to see his dad cry over this. He needs to learn from you how to grieve—that sometimes you've got to be strong enough to weep."

As if he had been given permission, the firefighter's eyes filled, and the tears spilled down his face. Then, from deep inside came a sob followed by another and yet another, his shoulders heaving as they continued coming. Ryan put a hand on his shoulder to comfort him, and the firefighter collapsed into his arms. Now the chaplain was weeping as well, and so were we all. Everyone. We were all hiding it, but we were all crying. It was a powerful, intimate scene, one that spoke of the experience like no other could.

This is what it is like for emergency service workers—the

firefighters, the police officers, and the emergency medical tech-
nicians (EMTs) who give all they have to disaster work. It is also
what it is like for a crisis chaplain. During disaster work, there is
always one hallowed moment that gives the chaplain a special
sense of why he or she is there. If the journey is made for no
other reason than to meet that person and that need, the trip
would be worthwhile. This was such a moment for my team
member. This was Ryan's "win."

How do you do it? people ask. My question is, How does
anyone do it?

My goal as a crisis chaplain had always been to show the
compassionate side of God in crisis, to be a tangible reminder of
a personal, loving God—to light a match in the midst of darkness.
Really, it seems a paradox. A place created by so much evil is the
last place most people think a God of love would be. It's certainly
the last place most *people* would want to be. But where else should
we be?

From those first moments inside the ground zero site, I knew
the only way the rage and horror would not overpower any good
I could do was to consciously keep my focus on an eternal
perspective. Working on the pile, I already sensed, would be overwhelming. Digging through sixteen acres of utter destruction all
but represented futility. If we as a nation didn't respond, though,
it would be as if we were saying we accept evil and nothing can
be done about it.

But there was also something else that kept the futility at bay
for me. In addition to the dignity of life provided by my helping

to recover the victims, I believed I was part of a bigger story being told by a Creator who deals in restoration, a story that started with the story of Christ, God's greatest redemption story. God never changes; in times of crisis, God waits to work through the losses in our lives. I believed that this story, begun on a beautiful September morning, was a tragedy—but a tragedy from which God wanted to redeem every part. I'm fairly certain of my heart's condition without the Christ story's effect on my own life; I know I would not have been standing in ground zero. I'd have been busy chasing my own goals, which would never have included helping people at a disaster site. But I have been so moved by the love and grace I've seen in my own life that the feeling propels me into trauma situations in hopes of helping others feel the same comfort. It's a powerful, powerful thing. And it is nothing but a humbling privilege to be a possible part of the redemption story in another person's heart. I cannot speak for others' reasons for why or how they do it, but that is mine.

Yet for the first few days at ground zero, I must confess that my efforts to fend off the anguish pouring from the atrocity surrounding me would be a struggle. So, purposely, from that first night, I resolved not to look at the rubble. I would force myself to look at the faces, to focus on seeing life, not death. And when I did look at the ruins, I would look for God in it—and, remarkably enough, the rubble itself did just that for many of the workers during the earliest days.

There was a place the workers called "God's House" within one of the caved-in buildings of ground zero. Inside what was left of the U.S. Customs building was a small miracle that everyone held on to during those first few weeks. A construction worker had stumbled onto it. A part of the north tower, Tower One, had fallen through the roof of the Customs building, creating a crater-sized hole all the way into the sublevels. Spray-painted arrows led inside, winding in and around the ruins; the floors above and below were compromised, and the surrounding din was loud, loud, loud—deafening to the point of pain. But with a step inside this interior area, its roof open to the sky, nothing but an unearthly quiet was heard. And there, rising from the despair, were three broken girders standing against the twisted, crushed wreckage of the building's offices. And they were, all three, broken off in the shape of crosses—distinct and heartbreaking.

Could I explain such a thing away? Of course. Should I? The workers answered those questions by naming the place and by returning to it, en masse, to reflect, to weep, and to pray despite the apparent danger. And I know why. Words almost fail me when I say this—but upon my first visit, standing there, looking down on those broken crosses, the rage subsided for a moment, and I felt a tremendous peace, the kind one describes as God's presence. Simply, quietly, in that still place, in the twisted structure, I was given a simple hiatus from rage—a reminder of sorts: *I'm still here, I'm still in this place. Look at these things.*

After that experience, even when the rage would wash over me, whenever I gazed past the people to the pile, I saw something new. Something about the skeletal girders still standing reminded me of the images I'd seen of ancient cathedrals standing broken but resolute during the world wars. The smoke, the play of light on the wreckage of steel pillars, the great, massive shadows cast, all spoke of some profound survival. And I didn't see broken beams anymore. I saw how the girders' joints created crosses wherever I needed to look.

THROUGH THE COURSE OF THE NIGHT, we had worked our way around to the decontamination area near the harbor where volunteers were rinsing down workers' boots, gloves, masks, and helmets as we came off the pile. Our twelve-hour shift was over, and we headed back to Homeport on police boats. We had traveled seventeen hours from California then ridden another two hours to Staten Island. We had talked to firefighters all night and then had gone to ground zero for twelve hours more. We had yet to sleep.

At 3 A.M. we were finally back at the Staten Island relief center.

As soon as we stumbled inside, exhausted to the bone and soul, Ronnie and her crew were waiting. "Everybody back outside," she said. "We've got a surprise!"

Outside, the volunteers, holding candles, had lined up to form the letters USA. And as they lit their candles, we all began to sing "God Bless America."

It was beyond glorious. It was home. At Homeport.

BACK INSIDE, I HEADED TOWARD the field first aid unit being manned by volunteer doctors and nurses. I've learned in disaster situations that Rule #1 is to take care of yourself—or else. While working a disaster site, we don't eat or sleep a lot, so we have to force ourselves to drink a lot of water and to take advantage of the available medical help. And eye care is first on my list. A doctor gently squeezed saline wash into my eyes, and a startling amount of black particles from the night washed out. Both the doctor and nurse made a point to comment on it while glancing back and forth from me to the gunk and back again, as if picturing where my eyes had been. The nurse even shook her head in wonder.

Disaster relief sites are always the epicenter of volunteer energy. It is a wonder to watch, as well as a blessing to receive. The Red Cross and Salvation Army relief centers are most famous for this kind of aid. Both agencies were doing what they do best, appearing all but instantly after a disaster, setting up centers, handing out aid, and coordinating the mass of volunteers who want desperately to be of use.

And every action, large or small, allows the volunteer to be connected in a personal way with the relief work. The man who washed your boots, the woman who served your meal, the doctor who cleaned your eyes, all feel like they've been there with you, and you feel the same way. The best example of this volunteer energy I had ever experienced was now embracing us at Homeport. These volunteers were doing it without any trained, experienced staff, and they were doing it twenty-four hours a day, seven days a week. I had no doubt that every weary disaster worker felt as I did about them that night—as if they were earthly angels hovering near to serve.

And these angels were ready to dish out the food when we were ready to eat it. At 4 A.M. they were lined up, waiting to feed their rescue workers. They had pot roast; they had casseroles; they had macaroni; they had sausages, chicken, and hot dogs. Every comfort food anyone could surely want—except for one.

As much as I tried, I didn't see what I suddenly had to have.

"Whaddya need, Fathuh?" Ronnie asked me in that wonderful Staten Island accent of hers.

"How 'bout peanut butter and jelly?" I asked. "Do you have that?"

"You want peanut butter and jelly, we'll get you peanut butter and jelly. Hey, everybody! The fathuh, he wants peanut butter and jelly!"

Within seconds, a group of Homeport earthly angels had converged on me.

"Which would you like, strawberry jelly or maybe you want grape jelly?" one woman asked.

"Maybe he wants jam or preserves," another said. "You want preserves, Fathuh?"

"What kind of bread you want, Fathuh?" yet another asked. "You want white, wheat, we got sourdough . . . How about on a roll? Would you like it on a roll?"

And then it was back to Ronnie. "What kind of peanut

butter, Fathuh? We got Skippy, we got Jif. We got chunky, no chunky. You like a lot of peanut butter and a little jelly or the other way around? How many do you want? Two? Three? You know what," Ronnie added, "we've got to have peanut butter and jelly sandwiches up here every night!"

She and her volunteer food crew had the whole place turned upside down, getting me my peanut butter and jelly. And I didn't dare stop them. I would have never said, "Oh no, please, don't go to any trouble," because this was how they were serving. These Staten Island citizens were being connected in the only way they could, and it moved me deeply.

As I downed my first sandwich, Ronnie asked, "Why is that your comfort food?"

"Because it represents innocence, I guess," I answered. "It's a kid's meal. And I just want to be innocent right now." It was wonderful to be that transparent with this Homeport angel. I felt safe enough with her to do that. This high-energy, can-do woman was ministering to me. It was the best peanut butter and jelly sandwich I ever had in my life.

FINALLY, KNOWING I HAD TO try to rest, even though I knew I probably would not be able to fall asleep, I headed for my air mattress. And there, lying on it, was a homemade card with what looked like a preschooler's lettering and art. On every cot and mattress within view lay similar cards.

"T-a-n-k, y-u," my card said underneath drawings of a fire-house and an American flag.

As I reflected on the images of those acts of people that to me reflected the face of God, I wrote an e-mail home on my Palm Pilot. Then I closed my eyes, with the little card still in my hand, and I slept for several hours.

September 19, 2001

. . . It was a long night at ground zero. Pictures can't describe it. Some things look like the face of pure evil. And yet other things remind me of the love of God. Like:

1. *The cards and letters from people around the world.*
2. *The generosity of people across the nation.*
3. *The commitment of people throughout this city.*

Chapter **Four**

Locked in a Memory

September 20, 2001

. . . Around the perimeter of ground zero, people just stand and watch. As I walk up Broadway, every few feet I am stopped by someone wanting to talk or to pray.

THE NEXT DAY, we went back to ground zero with the Homeport firefighters. After a few hours of talking with new firefighters waiting to work on the pile, I decided I wanted to get a sense of what the people coming down to ground zero were experiencing. I decided to take a few walks outside the perimeter when I had the chance, but first, I felt we needed to make our presence official and told one of the battalion chiefs so.

"Badges? How many do you need, Chaplain?"

He assigned a lieutenant to take me to the OEM, the Office of Emergency Management command center. This would be the first of four such trips during my work there, since the badges were updated periodically as part of security measures. We moved through the heart of ground zero and came out on the West

Highway. As far as I could see were mobile command centers lining the street, sidewalk, and median. There were units for an alphabet soup of agencies working with the disaster: FEMA, FBI, ATF, EMS, IRS, FDNY, NYPD, OEM, Corps of Engineers, Red Cross, Salvation Army, Coast Guard, Secret Service, Treasury Department, Customs, and at least a dozen more. There was even a mobile veterinarian clinic as well as a human first aid station. It was a strange sight, like some disaster bazaar.

As I was being escorted toward the OEM unit, I noticed the base camp for the New York USAR, the urban search and rescue team. I had been looking for this team since arriving, wondering if they were operational again after losing so many members.

"Can we stop for a minute?" I asked the lieutenant.

"Sure, Chaplain, let me take you in," he said.

As we pulled back the tarp entrance, I saw three members of the squad at a table planning the next tactical phase while a few others were taking a nap, stretched out on the floor. It had been six years since I had seen this unit at Oklahoma City. I feared all the ones I knew had died in the towers' collapse. But although we were all older and grayer, I recognized several of the squad immediately, and they recognized me.

We visited for a few minutes, talking about the disaster, about the members who were missing. Then, after inviting me to work with them and to bunk down there if needed, they said good-bye.

As we left, I was overwhelmed with the emotion of seeing some of these men alive. The command centers seemed to stretch on forever. There were so many more than I'd seen at Oklahoma

City. "You know," I said to the lieutenant, "we are getting way too good at this."

After making our team "official" with the appropriate number of clearance badges, we returned to the heart of ground zero. From there, I and one of our volunteer chaplains headed for Broadway, one of the other perimeter roads of the fenced-off district.

The number of people standing along the exterior perimeter with video and pocket cameras was startling. There were so many that I heard, more than once, other visitors taking loud exception to people treating the site as a tourist attraction. A few were even taking photos of me as I passed, some graciously asking, some not. Be it good taste or bad, the public was not to be denied its connection to the event. In fact, there would be a place on the West Highway dubbed "Point Thank You"—and the highway itself would be rechristened the "Hero Highway" because so many people would come there to shout encouragement to any and all workers that passed by, including the Teamsters driving dump trucks. Later I would tell everyone, "If you don't need to go, don't go," but at that moment, I could understand the need to see in order to believe, especially for New Yorkers.

We had only taken a few steps outside the checkpoint when we overheard a young woman arguing with the policeman who was guarding that part of the cordoned-off area. She was hysterical.

"You have to let me in! I have to go home! I don't have anywhere else to go. I don't have any family or friends in the city, and I don't even have a job anymore—it was in there, too! What am I supposed to do? Please let me go in!" she kept repeating.

I walked up to the police officer, who looked as if he was at his wit's end. "Can I help?" I asked him. After getting his permission, I began talking to the woman. She explained that she lived only a few steps from where we stood.

"I'm just losing hope every single day," the woman gasped. "This thing just doesn't go away. It doesn't end." Her situation became quickly clear. More than a week had passed since the event. She was like everyone else who lived in the area. Most had run for their lives, and everyone else was immediately evacuated, forced to literally drop everything and go. Now they could not retrieve even the basics they needed from their homes, and that included pets. One of the quiet heroics performed during the earliest days was the effort of the city's Humane Society volunteers and staff braving the area to rescue trapped animals.

This woman, however, did not even have a pet. She had fled her office and her home that September 11 morning with only what she had on her back. And now, unable to locate any of her fellow workers and having no one to turn to in the city, she could not even file for unemployment benefits for a job that no longer existed without retrieving documents from her abandoned apartment.

During the chaos of those first few days, there were many such stories. A mass of Red Cross volunteers wearing clearly marked vests and hats were walking the streets, attempting to identify the thousands who had been displaced just like this woman—stunned, and with every reason in the world to be hysterical.

Officials, I had been told, were having lots of problems identifying those who legitimately needed access into the area. Many people, strangely enough, couldn't prove their addresses. Unlike most adult Americans, many New Yorkers don't drive, so they have no driver's licenses to serve as routine IDs. Displaced students of several Lower Manhattan colleges were the best example of this problem. The only identification many had with them was a student ID with no real address, dorm room or otherwise.

This young woman, however, was obviously legitimate. I asked the police if she could go to her apartment, which was within a few yards of where we stood. He agreed, and as we watched, she walked down the block and vanished inside her apartment's front door. Within a few minutes, she reappeared, holding a manila folder and looking much calmer. With thanks and a hug for the volunteer chaplain with me, she moved back through the checkpoint and into the crowd to start putting her life back together. I've often wondered if seeing her apartment, connecting to her home one more time before moving on, was what she needed much more than the contents of that envelope.

A surprising number of people, including children and the elderly, live in Lower Manhattan. The bulk of them, more than nine thousand, lived in the Battery Park neighborhood adjacent to ground zero. They were all evacuated. The area's elementary schools were closed indefinitely, as were the nearby parochial schools. The impact on these children, many who were eyewitnesses to the attack, will be years in assessing. All the residents were forced to either leave the city or stay in nearby hotels. Some of Lower Manhattan's fanciest hotels cut prices and even changed gourmet restaurant menus to cater to these stranded families. Those families were the lucky ones, of course. Bus drivers would tell me about the regular riders who didn't get on their buses anymore. One driver mentioned the number of moving vans he'd seen—packing up those who had chosen to leave the city permanently, but most poignantly, packing the belongings of people who no longer lived anywhere.

As we walked down Broadway, the throngs of people everywhere I looked amazed me. Only a few feet from ground zero's death and grief, the city was filled with life and compassion. Because of my boots, gear, and helmet, those I passed knew I'd been down in the pile. And because of my clergy collar, people were approaching me, just as they had since Las Vegas. Most of those who stopped me were asking for prayer about what they feared could still happen, afraid the worst was yet to come. The anthrax scare had just begun; the fear of biological warfare was on everyone's minds. Anything seemed possible; anything we could imagine, we believed that a terrorist somewhere could imagine and act upon. Calming fears as best I could was a large part of my walks that day. But a few wanted to tell me their stories, stories the tellers themselves were sometimes struggling to believe.

One woman, during one of my later walks, shared her experience in a rush of words. On September 11, she was commuting from New Jersey on the subway that runs underneath the Hudson River to a station underneath the World Trade Center. She took an earlier train than she normally would have. And because she did, she stepped out of the subway train and onto the underground platform just as the first plane hit.

She and her fellow passengers suddenly found themselves unable to exit. Although she didn't know why at the time, the plane's impact had cut off the power. The subway gates had locked down.

People didn't know what to do; the crowd around her was beginning to panic, crushing up against the locked gates, pushing harder and harder against each other as more people got off the trains—and more trains arrived. She was in grave danger of being trampled.

"I know this sounds crazy," she told me, "but you of all people should understand. You see, I felt I literally heard God say to me, 'Turn around, stay to the left, and don't look back.' " As she began to do exactly that, she realized she would be able to go almost a quarter-mile underground if she continued to walk away from the exit. And she was amazed to see that her way was clear—there were no crowds coming the opposite way since no one was able to enter the subway station, either.

In New York City, during a normal rush hour, so many people are moving at the same time that order can only be kept if everyone walks on the right. That was, by habit, what everyone was still doing, even as panic set in. As she walked back into the subway system, walking cautiously on the left, she discovered that the subway exits had clamped closed all through the World Trade Center area. Not one of the passengers getting off the still-arriving trains could get out, and the mass of people had nowhere to go. The situation worsened with every passing second. She saw people pushed down and into walls by hysterical passengers. And yet she stayed to the left and was able to rush past them.

One moment haunted her most of all: A baby stroller was knocked over by the chaotic moving mass of people, and the baby fell out. But the hysterical mother didn't stop. Mercifully, a man scooped up the baby as the crowd kept rushing by.

Blocks and blocks later, still underground, she finally found an entrance that was open, and she rushed toward the daylight. To her horror, people were still entering the subway system. She tried to warn those passing her but was cursed, ignored, and pushed aside. Finally, at street level, in the sunlight again, she moved under a nearby steel awning and looked up at the World Trade Center—just as the second plane hit.

I would hear many eyewitness accounts of those harrowing hours, of being late to work that morning, of narrow escapes from falling debris, of unseen hands guiding lost survivors through darkness. And all the stories I heard that day would be told against a backdrop of a city adorned with homemade memorials to those who did not survive. In fact, such memorials began almost directly on top of ground zero itself. The firehouse quartered at the World Trade Center area, Engine 10, stood within the interior perimeter, its building damaged but still standing, supported by scaffolding. Dangling from the scaffolding and taped to almost every inch of the firehouse's exterior space were cards, letters, flowers, candy, and even teddy bears sent from around the country and the world, displayed solely for the benefit of the relief workers.

In fact, the entire barricaded perimeter, be it chain-link fence or police barricade, was adorned with such expressions of support. Whichever way you looked along the perimeter of ground zero, people had placed flowers, wreaths, and pictures of loved ones, as well as drawings and letters by the score. Near the decontamination area by the harbor, where I had been the night before, the existing granite police memorial dedicated to New York Police Department officers who had died in the line of duty had been transformed into a shrine to the fallen heroes of September 11. It was a sight to behold, and would continue to be so for months and months.

Only a block from the checkpoint, a tiny, ancient-looking church abutted ground zero. St. Paul's Chapel is its name, and something quite special happened there in the days immediately after September 11. The historic Episcopal chapel, so old that George Washington's pew is labeled, had somehow survived the collapse of the towers undamaged. Many Lower Manhattan houses of worship did not. St. Nicholas Greek Orthodox Church is one example of a church destroyed by the towers' debris. In contrast, the cemetery adjoining St. Paul's Chapel seemed to be the only part of its tiny grounds marred by the event; the green grass and ancient trees, as old as the nation itself, were covered with inches of soot, ash, and confetti-shreds of paper. But the rest of the chapel grounds was a wonderful mass of color and life. Its fence line, like the ground zero boundary behind it, held home-made signs of every kind, from missing-person posters to schoolchildren's banners. On its front steps, stockbrokers in expensive suits dished out food for the workers while along the front sidewalk, street artists created and shared their unique memorials of the event.

Inside the chapel, the scene was even more of a surprise. The sanctuary's walls, freshly painted a day before the attack, I was told, were now littered with letters, drawings, banners, and cards from around the world, taped directly to the new paint. The *New York Times* would later call the messages "impromptu wallpaper" that "tired, discouraged workers" could read for "emotional re-fueling." And I was one of those workers. One letter written by an eight-year-old is seared into my memory: *"If I'm ever left in a deep, dark hole,"* he wrote, *"I hope you'll be my hero and come find me, too."* I found it hard to take my eyes off those letters and cards along the walls. But when I did, I saw rescue workers sleeping and resting on the old wooden pews; one, I noticed, had stretched out on George Washington's pew.

Sanctuary. We refer, without thought, to the interior of our churches with that old, wonderful word. It comes from a role the church once played centuries ago, especially during wars. It was a refuge, a haven, a place to ask for asylum. The interior of St. Paul's Chapel, its sanctuary, became exactly that, a refuge for the relief workers. No photography was allowed. The lights were dimmed. Only the workers were let inside. The sanctuary was theirs. And its atmosphere exuded tranquility. They could rest, get a massage, be fed, or see a nurse, chiropractor, or podiatrist, all to strains of classical music played by volunteer violinists, cellists, and flautists.

All the respite centers were wonderfully diverse. The Red

Cross had established two centers near ground zero, one at the nearby Marriott hotel and another at the St. John's University complex. Both provided a full range of services and bustled with activity.

The Salvation Army first worked from a rustic tent on the West Highway median strip two blocks from ground zero's inner perimeter. Southern Baptist volunteers offered to cook for them, so the atmosphere was down-home friendly. Later, the Salvation Army would move to the thirty-one-thousand-square-foot tent by the harbor built by the Environmental Protection Agency as the decontamination center.

Near the harbor, St. Joseph's Catholic Church was the site for a center run by the Catholic Church, the Police Officers for Christ, and Calvary Chapel to meet the needs of the recovery workers. Nino's, a Lower Manhattan restaurant that became famous for offering thousands of free meals a day to police officers immediately after the attack, provided the food service.

St. Paul's Chapel, however, part of the parish of the much larger Trinity Episcopal Church only a few blocks south, offered the workers something that fed a different hunger, adding to a sense of historic survival for those who sought respite there. The historic church exuded an unspoken feeling of patriotism in the shadow of an act of war. It was a tiny stronghold of living history that had withstood more than two centuries of New York City development. It had survived every war the United States had ever fought. Such solidity and history nurtured us as much as the gentleness of its volunteer staff. I returned there often during the autumn of 2001. Although I spent only minutes at a time there, the peace felt like hours of care.

Rather than close the chapel and protect its historic interior from what one reporter vividly described as "the effects of hell being visited on the earth," its priest threw the doors wide open and, without governmental help, began serving all who entered—and soon, relief workers exclusively. It was my sanctuary of prayer, praise, tears, and rest on many of the nights I worked nearby.

I wasn't alone. In the days ahead, so many people would gravitate to this chapel on their American pilgrimages to ground zero that volunteers, including many of the visitors, would be put to work manning long scrolls of white paper, handing out pens and inviting one and all to express their thoughts. It was a good idea. This disaster touched us all; everyone needed a way to express his or her feelings. Soon St. Paul's would begin creating an archive of the scrolls and the correspondence, ever mindful of its place in history, then and now.

I left St. Paul's, after my first visit that afternoon, and followed a trail of posted messages away from the church, reading, one by one, the pieces of paper taped to fence posts, fire hydrants, subway entrances, and the like. Missing-person notices were, of course, the most heart-wrenching. Throughout the weeks ahead, I would see the missing-person posters almost everywhere I walked. In subways, on television vans, outside hospitals. The train stations were littered with them, each one breaking my heart anew. One is forever etched in my mind: A family photo with the father circled—*Have you seen our dad? Call this phone number, please!* By now, for all but the family members still clutching the comfort of denial, the reality was slowly settling in—these loved ones would not be found alive. The missing-person posters, though, remained as reminders of all the city had lost.

The excruciating sadness of each missing-person plea, though, was matched by the outpouring of encouragement and thanks and love exuded by all the handwritten correspondence from across America and around the world. The World Trade Center had been aptly named; citizens from eighty-two countries had died in the attack.

How did the letters get to this street? I saw messages from Germany, from France, from Italy, from Australia, from small towns across the USA—as small as a postcard and as big as a banner—saying, Thank you so much for being here; Thank you, rescue teams; Thank you, firefighters; Thank you, construction workers; Thank you, soldiers.

A young child had drawn a plane flying into a sad-faced building that was crying a teardrop; beside it was a flag-draped firehouse with a big, happy face. An older child had written intimate words to unknown readers: *Dear Firemen, I have a friend and her dad was in the building. It's hard right now but what really helps us is that you're there and you're still searching for him. Thank you so much.*

I always have to be careful at an event like this not to tarry in front of such cards and pleas, because I can only read so many before I start tearing up. And yet, doing so has always been the way I have found release when the stress becomes too much. In Oklahoma City, I often visited the card wall established at the site for that very reason. In Manhattan, the streets, the walls, the lamp-posts, the fencing—all were "card walls" of this disaster.

I found out, much later, how the messages had found me and everyone else around ground zero. As the messages came pouring into the city's fire stations, police stations, churches, and the mayor's office, volunteers had posted them wherever they believed the relief workers might see them. As I walked, passing block after block of these posted bits of encouragement, I began to feel the accumulated power of the messages and the wisdom of those who continued to display them.

There's something special about Americans. My upbringing in Europe has allowed me a perspective that most Americans don't have about themselves. We are different than people of other countries in more ways than a declaration of independence can convey. For all our faults, there's something unique about United States citizens, something about our resolve and compassion, our inner strength and grace under pressure.

I had seen it at other disasters, the way we pull together and the natural kindness we have for each other in such times. Here I was seeing such expressions multiplied by thousands. In what other country would people drop what they were doing and head straight for a place that had just been attacked by terrorists? Thousands of Americans did just that. Add the millions of those who prayed, who wrote cards and letters, and who gave more than $150 million during one weekend—a reported total of nearly $500 million from individuals, corporations, and foundations by year's end—and the point is made even stronger.

Volunteers of all shapes, all sizes, all races, and all religious faiths, from across the street and across the continent, came looking for a place to connect by looking for a place to serve. They hooked up with the Red Cross, the Salvation Army, with a local church or synagogue, ready and willing to do something—anything. Every imaginable donation was given, every service rendered, from giving blood to serving up free gumbo. The outpouring reminded me of the source of America's famed resilience. It comes from our "melting pot" and the tolerance it demands. I recall a wonderful quote about New Yorkers made by Mayor Rudy Guiliani in a *Life* magazine tribute: "Every day, we in New York City provide living proof that Christians, Muslims, Jews, Hindus, and Buddhists can live side by side . . . under one flag, in a spirit of mutual respect."

One of the most touching volunteer duties was performed by Red Cross volunteers who spent the first few days after the attack walking Muslim children to school. In certain parts of New York City, where Muslims feared being terrorized, volunteers not only escorted Muslim children to school but also went to the market for Muslim women who were afraid to leave home.

The Salvation Army was waiting outside the zone in strategically placed tents, the Red Cross had turned a dinner cruise ship, docked in the harbor, into an early respite center, and McDonald's displayed corporate volunteerism by feeding the waiting firefighters hamburgers and fries. To hear "Do you want fries with that?" as we were standing near a million pounds of twisted girders was a uniquely American experience, to say the least.

The volunteers themselves often brought stories of their own when they showed up to help. The staff at St. Paul's found these people and their stories a "source of amazement," as a *New York Times* profile expressed it. One of the first to respond, for instance, had been an elderly woman who told them she had come all the way from the Bronx to donate her cane because she heard someone had a leg injury.

Why do we want to help? What fuels this volunteer urge? No one asks this question; we simply take for granted our impulse to offer aid and comfort after tragedy strikes. I believe the reason has something to do with the way we are put together. New Yorkers expressed a helplessness that they could only salve by "plugging in," as one New Yorker put it. God made us to be connected, to be a part of a community, despite the American rugged individualism that's so much a part of our national psyche. In the aftermath of tragedy, people seem to naturally return to their basic God-designed programming, to the way their hearts are wired. This dynamic was also what fueled the firefighter and police officer devotion to duty that we all now honor as heroic. It is surely the same impulse that inspires rescue workers to call each other "brother" or "sister."

For a Christian chaplain, the dynamic also includes being there to offer the comfort of a spiritual connection, the love of God we know because of Christ. As Mother Teresa often explained her work's motivation, the Christian chaplain is there to "offer a cup of cold water in Jesus' name." I've experienced the love of that spiritual connection in a powerful way myself. So, while I work as a crisis chaplain to meet the pressing physical and emotional needs of trauma victims, I want to offer that enormous spiritual comfort as well, helping hurting hearts connect with the heart of God in whatever way I can. But the same is true for "volunteer" chaplains as well.

Proper professional credentials are mandatory for the level of work I do; certifications, training, and the like are all needed as competency fail-safes and are recognized by federal and city agencies. The World Trade Center disaster site became a magnet for all sorts of groups more interested in photo opportunities or proselytizing than crisis intervention work. Most were well-meaning but lacked an understanding of the dynamics involved; their focus was misguided at best, harmful at worst. Professional credentials are essential in chaplaincy work.

For nonprofessionals interested in compassionate crisis care, however, one crucial credential compels the most effective service. Like basic volunteerism, basic compassionate crisis work begins with a matter of will but follows through with a matter of heart.

I often say, "If I have nothing else to give, I can give the gift of presence." Skills are never the issue. If a volunteer is able to give his or her heart, is willing to be present with crisis victims, then the volunteer can learn the skill of "attention"—how to be in tune with people's specific needs. This skill can be taught—what to say, what not to say, how to listen, when to offer a tissue or a cup of cold water, how to interpret body language, when to hug or touch a shoulder. We've been training people for years in private, corporate, and church settings to meet the needs of everyday community crises. The right heart, however, is something a person either has or doesn't have. God chooses to work through "flesh suits," as I often call us flawed, fragile human beings, for reasons the Creator of the universe only knows. And the first thing we "flesh suits" must do is be willing to be there. That is the first stage of what we call "a ministry of presence." Everything begins with being there and being willing to learn how to be alert, in tune with the specific needs of the moment, be they physical, emotional, or spiritual.

So for the volunteer with that heart who approaches our organization desiring to learn how to be something special for people in crisis, I have always had a basic philosophy. I say, "C'mon. Let's go." The team members who accompanied me on the original New York trip began as just such volunteers. One went to Homeport and ground zero with me; the other stayed with the Manhattan church that had invited us to help coordinate the flood of disaster needs facing its staff.

Such heart isn't reserved for large, mass disasters. Anyone, everyone, can be a "chaplain" on some level to the victims of crises in his or her spheres of influence. There are tragedies every day happening all around us. In fact, that is how I first began this work. In 1987 I had seen the newspaper headline reporting the tragic deaths of the two small boys who were hit by a car while riding a tricycle. It had caught my eye and my heart. I suddenly wondered who was helping their single welfare mothers with the practical matters of the tragedy. Who was helping them pick up the pieces, bury the boys properly, cope with the arrangements and the costs?

I found out the answer—no one was helping them. No social services can meet all the needs of the traumatized. They were about to fall through the cracks of society's official safety nets.

Our modern, mobile culture leaves many of us a long way from the safety nets of community, church, and family. So I volunteered the day I read about the two little boys. We Care, our organization providing compassionate crisis care, was begun that simply. Our compassionate Christian social work began slowly to fill a growing gap in crisis care, and the work ultimately included the nation's escalating number of mass tragedies, from school shootings to terrorist bombings. That is why my heart cheered for every volunteer I met in New York City.

I stopped for a moment on the corner of Broadway and Church, where a young street artist was giving out copies of a drawing. He handed me one . . . It depicted a firefighter kneeling over a victim, and standing over the firefighter was an image of an angel.

DURING MY WALKS THAT DAY and the days to come, I began approaching others as naturally as people were approaching me, being very sensitive to whether I was invading their space. That was how I met a man near the perimeter fence. He looked dazed, glassy-eyed. It was the same look a deer has when caught in head-lights on a country road, eyes vibrant but body frozen to the spot.

All along the perimeter fencing, I had seen people with this look. They seemed almost catatonic, hypnotized by the pile loom-ing more than twenty stories high. So many people in and around the ground zero site were in this state, it had become dangerous. More than once, I'd had to pull a person out of harm's way.

"Hey, a truck's coming," I'd yell. "Hey, hey, pay attention there!"

They didn't seem conscious of their whereabouts. It was as if they were locked in a memory.

That was how this man seemed. So I approached him to see if I could help in some way. At first his only response was odd: "Why did I stay back?"

Finally I learned his story. He was a port authority officer who had been at ground zero that September morning. On his radio, he could hear fellow officials high in the Twin Towers telling other port authority employees to stay put, that the fire would be contained. Some of their offices were on the highest tower floors.

But he was outside seeing the reality of the situation far better than his colleagues inside. Frantically, he began to call into his radio, "No, no! It's not safe! Get out! Get out!" And he continued his warnings until it was too late.

Now, like many of the firefighters, he was living in a strange paradox. He would have rather gone into the buildings to help, even if it meant he would have died.

"At least I would have done something," he said.

"But you did do something," I told him. "Had you run in, you wouldn't have been able to understand the scope and the

80

immediate sense of danger the others were in. You'll never know how many people you saved by staying back and sounding the warning."

He looked at me as if he'd never considered what would have been obvious to anyone listening. Finally, with someone who was safe, he was allowing himself to process the facts of the events. He had been trapped in the recurring memory of the September 11 horror he had experienced. This may sound strange. After all, he had experienced the reality of that tragic morning more than a week earlier. But the mind plays self-defense tricks. It often retreats into denial in traumatic times, and the denial can take many forms. A person's "stuck" memory can create scenarios to match the occasion. Sometimes the person is trapped in guilt; other times in anger, or fear, or loneliness. A very common mental "loop" in a disaster setting is the one this man was forcing on himself—a superhero or rescuer-savior complex in which he believes he could and should have done more, when in reality he did all he could.

It's not uncommon for victims to be unable to access the memory correctly, even though they've lived it, until they are able to articulate it. The act of stating the experience out loud allows the person to truly cope with the traumatic event in a healthy way. And those who don't articulate the experience, who stay trapped in the memory, sooner or later will suffer all sorts of harmful reactions, physically, emotionally, and spiritually, ranging from nervous breakdowns to drug and alcohol abuse, in order to keep the pain at bay. Healing can only begin when the survivor begins to talk. So, in telling his story, the port authority officer was able to begin his personal process of healing.

Throughout the weeks ahead, I would see this dynamic occur over and over as I talked to survivors of the attack. Getting people to tell their stories allowed not just emergency service personnel but citizens on the streets, on trains, in restaurants, at universities, and in corporations to move forward, to unlock their minds from their 9/11 memories.

A detective named Beth was like that. I would meet her the next Monday morning at sunrise. As I was coming off an overnight shift, I saw a woman in her thirties ahead of me, leaning on a piece of construction equipment. She was wearing jeans and a detective's badge, but I still thought it was odd that she'd be there at that time of day. It had been a cold and rainy night. Sunlight had just come peeking through the buildings, and the sun was shining on her face in a golden way. She was soaking it in, sitting all by herself.

"Hey," I called to her, moving in on her sunshine. "Come on, share. I've been out here all night working. I'm cold and you're sitting in the best seat in the house, soaking up all the sun here."

She played right along, smiling at this crazy man wearing a clergy collar.

"You can share my sun any day, Chaplain," she said.

We chatted about nothing of consequence, just a little light conversation to go with the sunlit feeling. Finally I asked, "Beth, where were you when this happened?"

"I was right here," she said, "working in a triage area we'd set up. There were firefighters here with us, and we were all helping people who'd been hurt when the planes crashed into the towers." She paused, looking past me. "Until the building came down."

The force of the implosion blew her thirty yards, into a revolving door, along with two firemen who had instinctively covered her with their own bodies an instant before the blast.

"Do you know what happened to them?" I asked.

She sighed, shaking her head. "I never thanked them or saw them again. I know they lived through the blast because they rushed away. But when I turned around, I realized everyone else who had been near me in the triage area was somewhere under the collapsed building."

She had come every day since the attack, always to the same spot, always at the same time, trying to make sense of the senseless. Two questions haunted her: "Why did God allow this? And why did I live?"

Like the port authority officer, she was locked in a memory, returning again and again to the scene. In those first few days, I came to understand that part of my job was to get such people unlocked from their memory by listening. Most often, those in dire need of voicing their experience exhibited a certain faraway look, a preoccupation with a sight in their mind, much like the port authority officer had. Others, however, hid their preoccupation far too well. One such moment would take me by surprise.

When most of the Staten Island firefighters got off duty, they'd grab the ferry, a police boat, a harbor boat, a Coast Guard vessel, whatever was the fastest way home. At the end of the next day's work, I decided to go back with a couple of firemen on the Staten Island ferry. As we boarded the boat, a dignified woman in her mid-fifties in front of me asked who I was. I sat down with her, and for a few minutes we chatted. Then, silently, we both found ourselves staring back at the city's skyline, now forever changed. "There's such a gap in the skyline now," she finally commented. "As if the city's two front teeth have been knocked out."

Yes, I agreed. The sight was strange.

A quiet woman sat to my left, satchel in hand. She looked as if she had just finished her workday.

"How was your day?" I asked, introducing myself.

"It was my first day back," she answered with a slight smile.

"Really. How was it?"

"It was good," she answered.

"Where do you work?"

"I work in a high-rise building in Lower Manhattan."

"That must be hard. What did your company do for you?" I asked. I wanted to find out what the city's corporations were doing to help their employees cope, since I had been involved in such work. "Did they have some counselors there to help you work through what happened?"

"They had people there," she said and added almost more to herself, "but I have a plan."

Oh? I thought, *a plan. Plans are good.* "Tell me about it."

"No, I can't tell you. I can't talk about it," she murmured.

We had been seated side by side, and now, with the change in her voice, I turned toward her. She was crying. "It's a sin," she said. "I just can't tell you my plan; I just can't do it." And then she began to sob.

I put my arm around her. She didn't pull away; she was sobbing so deeply I suspected this was the first release she had allowed herself since the attack. But there was more, I could tell.

"Right here, you and I, right now," I said quietly, "we'll just have a little time of being with God. Nobody will know. It's just us two."

She told me her plan.

"I can't stand it any longer. I can't wait to have a plane hit our building and die like those people did, being burned, falling out of the buildings, being crushed . . . I know it's going to happen again. And I work up so high, just like those people did. So I've made up my mind. I'm going to go home tonight, and I'm going to get my daughter. I'm going to kill her, then I'm going to kill myself, because I want to be in control of how we go."

It took me a moment to grasp what this woman was thinking. It chilled me to the bone. I realized that she was convinced, stuck in the memory of what she had seen only days before, that more attacks were a certainty, and she would be as helpless in her office, high in the sky, as the original attack's victims had been. I couldn't suggest quitting her job or moving out of the city; she thought everything was going to be decimated—where she lived, where she worked, even where I lived and worked. The world was coming to an end, so there would be no safe place. She wasn't going to die in a fire, and she wasn't going to die falling out of a building. She was going to choose her end, and she was not going to leave her daughter to face the world's end alone.

For several more minutes, we cried together, we talked together, and we prayed together. Our talk wasn't a spiritual conversation as much as it was just a conversation about life. I worked hard to sound like a voice of reason, even as I knew I had not seen what she had. I contemplated what I should do. We only had a few minutes left before we docked. Then we arrived, and she quickly went her way before I could do anything at all. A couple of minutes later, as I waited at the curb for our ride, a car pulled up. From it, the woman suddenly appeared. I almost didn't recognize her. Her whole demeanor had changed. She rushed over and gave me a big hug. "Thank you so much," she said. "I want to live. Thank you for helping me."

She really didn't have to be talked out of her plan. It was as if once her idea hit the air, once she articulated her worst fears, she snapped out of it. It had scared her to be thinking it as much as it had scared me to hear it. Hearing her thoughts out loud became a sort of catharsis. She had been pulled out of her shock.

What would have happened if I hadn't been on that ferry and she hadn't decided to confide her plan to me? She might have been one of those people who "just snapped." And nobody would have known why.

I had seen such suicides. Tragic deaths can lead to other deaths, sometimes with no apparent warning. The first suicide in the wake of the World Trade Center attack would happen only weeks from that day. A fifty-one-year-old breast cancer survivor took her own life. Her husband had gone to work at the World Trade Center on September 11 and hadn't come home. All she had left was her precious dog and the mountain dream home she and her husband had built. She had seemed to be coping outwardly, much like the woman on the ferry. She had even orchestrated a memorial service for her husband near ground zero. But then, almost a month to the day after her husband died, her prized dog died of cancer. And she had taken a pistol and shot herself in the head.

The woman on the ferry could easily have become another surprising suicide.

But all she had needed was what all grieving people need. They need their stories validated by being heard. They don't need advice; they don't need lectures or sermons. They only need dedicated listeners: *Tell me your story. Let me hear it so you can hear it. Let's talk of divine love and encouragement, so you can move forward with healing hope into your life again.*

As the woman drove away from the ferry landing, I stood there for a long time before I could move. I recall a dawning awareness of my being part of something very special, something beyond anything I had ever experienced. I was a chaplain, after all. I had seen God at work in many lives through crises, but every nerve in my body told me something unique, something holy, was happening with this disaster. I had heard people from all walks of life refer to ground zero as consecrated, holy ground. I was beginning to feel that the meaning of those words was broader than any of us could imagine. I had been in New York such a short time and already I had seen remarkable moments that could only have come through the touch of the divine. I rarely sleep more than a few hours a day when I'm in a crisis situation, but now I found myself almost unable to close my eyes at all, wondering what would happen next.

September 20, 2001
. . . What about the thousands in Lower Manhattan that morning who weren't in the Twin Towers? Many were traumatized, nevertheless. They did not lose their lives, but a part of them died that day.

Chapter Five

Fresh Kills

September 21, 2001

AFTER FINALLY ARRIVING AT HOMEPORT, I knew I couldn't sleep. It was only 5:30 in the afternoon, so I went over to the food area to get a little dinner. There I met some New York Police Department officers who were part of the narcotics division assigned to Staten Island. Their offices were next to the Homeport Naval Station.

Because of my investigative background with law enforcement as well as my experience as a police chaplain, I feel a real kinship with police officers. Prior to going into crisis intervention work, I served with the state of California as a senior special investigator working on criminal cases, forgery prosecutions, unemployment disability insurance fraud, and other abuses against governmental systems. My job was to investigate then bring cases for prosecution to the district attorney's office. Later, in Sacramento, my partner, Jeff, and I had worked for a time with local law enforcement as chaplains. Through the aid of grants, we had participated in a program that trained chaplains to provide compassionate care and support on 911 calls.

I introduced myself to the policemen, and as we ate and chatted, we talked about where each of them had been when the planes hit the World Trade Center. When I asked what the worst part of the attack was for them, one officer's answer set my course for the night.

"The hardest part for us is tonight. We have to work at 'Fresh Kills,'" he said.

Fresh Kills? I hadn't heard the term. "You mean, ground zero?" I asked.

"No, Fresh Kills is the place we're dumping all the material from ground zero. They've opened up an old landfill here in Staten Island to put it all."

The debris trucked off the World Trade Center site, he explained, was being loaded onto a barge, ferried down the river to Staten Island, then hauled to the reopened landfill for processing. The "processing" was the final attempt to retrieve anything salvageable.

"We've been assigned to go there tonight and rake and dig," the officer went on. "And the even harder part of that is the fact that a son-in-law of one of the guys on our crew was in Tower One. And it's pretty certain he died there."

What the officer wasn't saying hovered there between us: The man might actually find his own son-in-law's remains.

"Is he here?" I asked.

They pointed to a man sitting at another table. I went over and introduced myself. "I'm sorry to hear about your son-in-law. I know you have to go do this tonight. How are you holding up?"

"I want to go," he answered. "I want to do something. I want to feel like I'm helping my family out there. And the other families, too. Whatever I can do . . . you know?"

I glanced back at the other police officers. I wasn't going to sleep; I knew that. And I had just lost any appetite I had mustered. I walked back to where they sat. "I'd like to go with you tonight out there. That okay?"

"Well, sure, Chaplain. Let's get the sergeant's okay."

The sergeant listened to my request, then he took me to his lieutenant.

"I want to go with you guys when you work tonight, if it's all right," I asked again.

"It's nasty, Chaplain; it's bad duty," he said. "You sure?"

"Yes," I said.

"Well, then, that'd be great."

They were about to leave, so I suited back up—my helmet, respirator, gloves, boots, and jacket, and since it had begun to rain again, I also put on warm clothing and my rain suit.

We piled into their undercover van and headed across the island. When we arrived at the landfill checkpoint, the driver rolled down his window. The smell was hideous. Being a retired landfill was enough to make the stench overpowering, but now it also had ground zero's odors added to the mix.

The police officers all presented their badges to the guard.

The guard leaned over and looked at me. "Well, who is this?"

"He's our minister," one of them said. "We brought our own because this is a scary place."

The checkpoint guard laughed. "You really want to go in here?" he said my way, then shook his head and waved us through.

Once inside, we all suited up in white decontamination suits as if we were going to the moon—from respirator masks to vinyl gloves to built-in boots. We all now looked alike, so someone began writing our names on the backs of our suits in case of an accident.

On mine, the man wrote "Chaplain Ray," putting crosses all over my back. Walking around toting a sign like that, I shouldn't have been surprised at the reaction of other workers. But I was. Every few minutes, someone expressed astonishment that a chaplain would want to be there.

"Where else would I be tonight?" I kept responding. "If the church is about people, you guys are people, right?"

As we moved toward the work area, one of my crew said, "Come on, Chaplain, you're going to get hurt in here."

Knowing cops as I do, I realized that they would be reserving judgment about me: *Let's really see what this guy is made of. Let's see if he really bends down and picks up a body part.* But that was fine, even expected. So I answered, "Hey, I'm with you tonight. We can go. But if you're going to stay, I'm going to stay."

This work was the ministry of presence in its purest form. When you've had a rake in your hands for twelve hours, sifting through the remains of a disaster, you have a perspective of what the workers saw, smelled, tasted, and felt, so that, later on, you can understand those workers in a way others cannot. If you had such an opportunity, then you'd be prepared when such a person arrived in your parish, your congregation, or your counseling office, trying painfully to express his experience, because you'd know exactly what he or she was feeling.

A machine near where we stood suddenly started up again, making a noise loud enough to pop an uncovered eardrum.

Clank. Clank. Clank. Clank.

"That's the sifter!" one of them explained to me over the din.

Large skip loaders were unloading debris into a gigantic sifting machine. The sound was being made by a constant tapping of the metal against the sides of the thing, separating the construction materials, the dust, and broken building fragments from everything else. The process was fascinating to watch, even in this grim setting. What the sifter left was dumped in small piles in an area lit up like daylight—pile after pile after pile. And along the row of piles stood a long line of other white suited personnel. Squads of six to twenty people were sifting through each one.

As we moved to our own pile and began to rake through it, I asked, "What are we looking for?"

"Whatever we can find!" someone yelled over the noise. "We're looking for anything to ID: body parts, personal items, airplane parts—anything."

"Does anybody know what airplane parts look like?" someone called out.

"No, but this guy over here says he's an expert, and when we see something, we'll ask him," came the answer.

That was the assignment for the night. Every time a plop of

material from the sifter came down in front of us, we pulled it apart. Then, when the pile had been thoroughly examined, everybody backed away and watched as another front loader pushed the remains over the hillside and into the landfill pit. And that was the end of the ground zero debris.

THE NEXT TWELVE HOURS were a space and time beyond words for me. That was where the disaster became far too real. At ground zero itself, even with the rage I felt at what I saw, I hadn't yet gotten a full sense of the perishing of lives. The ruined buildings were horrifically surreal, the soot covering every inch of ground was omnipresent, and the television images were forever etched in my mind's eye. But for all my feelings of anguish and anger, I had yet to see the recovery of a body. So the purest human reality of it—that people actually lost their lives—had not settled into my psyche, no doubt out of my mind's natural self-defense.

But when you are standing in a place called Fresh Kills, you're constantly reminded that you're dealing with the real deaths of real people. And soon I would know exactly what the rescue workers at ground zero must have gone through during the first few hours of the crisis.

The first identifiable item we found was a wallet. As one of the officers in our group pulled it out of our pile, everyone was thinking the same thing: *Whose is it?* We wanted to know, and we didn't want to know, considering our team member's missing son-in-law. The officer held it close until he was able to see the name inside the wallet—it wasn't the son-in-law's. Speculation then began. Had it been on the owner's person, or did he leave it behind when he ran for his life? It was totally intact; his driver's license, credit cards, even a few bills were still inside. But all I could picture was what it represented: a life.

At ground zero, I often heard first-time visitors comment on the absence of "things": Where are the computers? they would wonder. The furniture? Where is everything? Where are all the human-size objects that clutter daily life?

At Fresh Kills, poking through each new pile, we found them. A street sign, a vacuum cleaner, a coffeepot, a gold chain, law books. One of my most vivid recollections was finding two perfectly white, totally intact golf balls carrying the logo of a World Trade Center company. To see those golf balls so pristine they could have been teed up and driven on the fanciest of golf courses was beyond ridiculous. The way some things survived untouched when so much did not was truly bizarre. How fragile life is.

Then, suddenly, we found human remains.

When you work at disaster sites, you come to know some smells unmistakably. A cadaver has a rancid, putrid odor that is instantly recognizable.

When I was working as a police chaplain in Sacramento, the sheriff's office asked us to visit the mother of a missing boy. The sheriff's deputy assigned to the missing-persons unit wanted us to

95

prepare the mother for the worst, that he was probably not going to be found, and even if they did find him, he most likely would not be alive due to the torrid summer heat. The temperature had been more than a hundred degrees for several days. The deputy believed the boy had climbed into a garbage dumpster at the mall near his house. In the heat, he had gotten trapped then suffocated. They expected him to be found soon at the city dump.

On the way to the mother's house, I told my partner that, dead or alive, we should pray for some closure for the family as well as for the officer involved. Unresolved children's cases are perhaps the hardest for everyone. They haunt all involved for years.

After our visit with the mother, we were about to drive away when an elderly lady waved us down. "You have to help me," she said.

"What's the matter, ma'am?" I asked.

"I have a smell in my house."

"Where do you live?" I asked.

She pointed. The boy's mother lived in one side of a duplex building; the elderly lady lived in the other.

I told my partner I'd be right back.

As I passed through the doorway of her small duplex, the stink of a dozen odors hit me—birds, cats, soiled carpet, smoke, old wood. *Gee, lady,* I thought, *how can you tell one smell from another?* So I asked, "Which smell, ma'am?"

She pointed to the fireplace. She had made it into a makeshift altar complete with Virgin Mary statue and candles, all of which were burned entirely down. I tried to open the flue, figuring the candle fume was the problem. It wouldn't budge.

"Maybe you should keep this flue open," I suggested.

"The flue *is* open," she said.

"No ma'am, it's not."

"Son," she said, "I may be old, but I'm not crazy. That flue is always open because I burn those candles all the time."

I checked again.

Then I smelled it—the putrid stench of decomposition. I had smelled the odor before but never like this. I realized I had probably found the missing boy.

I asked my partner to call in the situation.

Within minutes, sheriff and fire personnel arrived with a ladder. A firefighter and I climbed onto the roof with a strobe light and headed to the elderly woman's chimney. One flash of the strobe showed us the awful truth—the boy was inside. Apparently, he had watched an episode of the television series *The X-Files* in which a humanlike monster had slid into a house through a chimney. The boy, in his innocence, had climbed onto the attached roof of the elderly neighbor's house and tried the stunt himself. He'd closed the flue with his foot and died inside.

Within a few hours, we had removed his badly decomposed body, all of us either puffing on cigars or rubbing Mentholatum under our nostrils to mask the smell in order to do the job.

The same type of scenario would be played out at Fresh Kills.

Earlier, at Homeport, I had noticed civilian crews of retired firefighters clipping cigars by the hundreds. I didn't have to ask what they were for. So the last thing I had done before heading to Fresh Kills was stuff my pockets with cigars from the Homeport stash. As odd as it sounds, the chaplain at Fresh Kills was the one passing out cigars. That alone had earned my place with the workers there. There weren't enough cigars in the world to rid the air of the stench, but what we had was enough to do what needed to be done.

At the first whiff of the smell coming from our pile, one of the members of the unit yelled, "Over here!" Trained police dogs were stationed nearby for such moments. They brought one of the dogs closer; everybody stepped back for its reaction. When the dog barked, we knew exactly where to look in our pile. We uncovered a piece of a hand.

As grotesque and horrific as the discovery may seem, such moments invoke a different emotion for the disaster worker. The hellish job becomes suddenly purposeful, giving a sense of meaning to the whole night. The work becomes a service in the most essential of ways. Identification of victims is important duty at any disaster but especially for this one, since so many bodies would never be found. Since the smallest bit of remains can now be matched for DNA, any such discovery means that a family will have some closure, just as it did for the missing boy's mother in Sacramento. And beyond that, anything we detected would also give one more family something to bless, bury, or memorialize, depending on their faith's beliefs about death.

The remain was placed into a five-gallon bucket that would ultimately be taken to a makeshift morgue to begin the process of identification, then we went back to the search.

We finished "processing" that rubble pile to the cacophony of the machine's *clank, clank, clank*. We stepped back and watched as the rest of the rubble was pushed over the side of the dark hill. Then another pile was plopped down before us.

We continued our grim business for the entire shift. As the night wore on, our soberness began to deepen—no one really talked at Fresh Kills beyond the most basic communication. But a crisis chaplain's presence goes beyond talking.

A chaplain in such a situation offers a "safe out" for these macho men who are still human, nevertheless. If the work becomes overwhelming, these workers don't have to go to the sergeant or the lieutenant; they can go to the chaplain. In fact, they only have to look at a chaplain as if to say, *Hey, I need to talk to you*. Then all I have to do is raise my hand and motion to a sergeant, which indicates that a worker needs a few minutes with a chaplain. Everyone in emergency service work understands that if he asks for a moment with the chaplain, it will be granted. If that moment is four hours or the rest of the night, no questions are asked. Workers are not going to lie to a chaplain. And every chaplain knows that being a "safe out" is the most basic of the many reasons he or she is there.

Another reason for a crisis chaplain's presence is the very fact of death. Why should we be there? Because death is there. When remains of any size are uncovered at a crisis site, even tough police officers will say, "Do we pray over it before we bag it? How do we pay respect?" That always seems to be the question, relief workers tell me. There's a protocol followed after such a find, but there is also, at the same time, an urge by the human beings who find it to offer some sort of respect for the life it held. This is why fire departments have chaplains. A chaplain's presence and the spiritual dimension it represents offers the chance to give humanity back to what death takes away. A crisis chaplain's presence gives relief workers the permission they fundamentally need to express dignity for life even after death. But beyond that is an even more basic reason for being there. Disaster workers want chaplains with them at places with such names as ground zero or Fresh Kills—on any rescue battlefield where they are looking death straight in the face.

WE FINISHED THE SHIFT about 7 A.M. and returned to Homeport. I showered as soon as I arrived. As hard as I tried, I couldn't quite wash the smell off my skin. I met the narcotics officers in Homeport's mess hall area. As we ate breakfast, we got to know each other and were able to laugh again, giving ourselves a chance to connect after the somber service we'd done together. To know I was a part of something sacred for them was now sacred to me.

When I finally lay down in an attempt to rest, I still couldn't shake the Fresh Kills smell. I got up and showered again, and soon realized that the smell wasn't on my skin but up my nose. I stood with my face under the shower, hoping that would get rid of the stench. When that didn't work, I went to see the nurse in the medical relief area. Could they somehow wash out my sinuses?

With a glob of Mentholatum, she swabbed out my nostrils as best she could. It helped, but didn't get rid of it all. Yet I didn't mind. To have been invited along by those police officers as they performed the hardest of "hard duty" had been a privilege.

CHAPTER **SIX**

God in the House

September 22, 2001

. . . People are asking questions about huge issues: Why did I live? Where was God when this happened? Will I ever stop hating? They come from the young and the old, from everyone and everywhere.

THE NEXT BUS TAKING THE fire squads to ground zero was leaving at 2 P.M., and I wanted to be on it. Sleep was out of the question, my adrenaline still in high gear. But I forced myself to rest awhile, then I caught the bus back to Manhattan.

If I ever forgot the global nature of the event, something each day would remind me. That weekend, it was seeing movie stars walk by while we waited for our turn on the pile. Native New Yorkers such as Susan Sarandon and Billy Joel would suddenly appear, signing hard hats and chatting with everyone they met. Seeing celebrities' well-known faces in such a place was at first strange, but it also made sense. This was their home, and that was their gift. Offering the gift of their famous presence to the rescue workers helped morale considerably.

That weekend was also the first time I ever saw humor used as an emotional coping mechanism at a disaster site. It was raining again. We all had our yellow suits on, waiting to go on the pile, when comedian Bill Murray walked up in a yellow slicker, his rain hat pulled down as far it would go, looking like he had just come off the set of his movie *What about Bob?* He ambled toward us, shoulders hunched up to his ears. He took one look at the rubble, then glanced back at us and said, "You know, you just can't get a good cup of coffee in this town anymore, can ya?" We all cracked up, and he shuffled down the line to do the same for the next group of rescue workers. I remember thinking, *What an interesting twist*. The nature of this event continued to bring out the most unique expressions of volunteerism.

After another twelve-hour shift of waiting and talking in the rain, then a few intense hours of fruitless digging, we returned to Staten Island about 2 A.M. It would be the last night we'd spend at Homeport. Things were already changing. The firefighters were slowing down their deployments out of Staten Island. The city's fire service was reducing the number of firefighters assigned to ground zero work so they could rest and be ready for the wakes and memorial services that were set to begin in the next few weeks. Rather than searching en masse, now they were going to be searching on a limited basis while performing service to the widows and the children, honoring the men who had died in the line of duty.

The last deployment to ground zero of Staten Island firefighters would be that night. So we knew we would not be returning to Homeport the next day. The relief center would stay open for the police officers working at Fresh Kills, as well as being a base for the growing number of National Guard troops moving in and out of the city. We felt, though, it was time to move on. Nearby Manhattan hotels had lowered their rates drastically, eager to help. So through the generous donation of our major corporate supporter, A. Teichert & Son Construction, we found housing a short subway ride from ground zero.

One of our immediate goals was to find the New York fire department's chaplains. There had only been a half-dozen for all fourteen thousand firefighters before September 11, and one of them had been killed in the first few moments of the disaster. So I had yet to talk with one. Finally I reached one of the senior chaplains by telephone. We offered to take the late-night watch— what I once called the graveyard shift, but no more. Firefighters called it "C-watch" or "third watch," and now so did we. I had noticed that very few chaplains were staying with the workers during this overnight shift. "We'd like to cover third watch for you, if that'd be okay," I said. He agreed immediately, thanking us.

After talking with him, I also realized why I had seen so few chaplains these first few days inside the ground zero area. Most of the support people that I had expected to be there had already put in a seven-day work effort before I arrived. Between a week and two weeks was a typical stay for most crisis workers who travel to a disaster. By the end of the second week, most out-of-town chaplains were at the end of the usual time of service. We had walked into the gap. If we had come right away, we would have been much less useful since hundreds of other chaplains would have also been there.

The scenario is not unfamiliar to crisis responders, nor to us during our earliest efforts. In 1991 a man shot twenty-three people dining in a Texas restaurant. He had driven his car through a plate-glass window and into a Luby's Cafeteria in Killeen, Texas, gotten out of the wrecked car, and opened fire. We Care had received a casual invitation to help, but nothing official. Yet we had gone anyway, as did many others, following the national news exposure, and we spent days wandering around looking for ways to help.

Finally we found our way to a tiny nearby town named Copperas Cove, which was the home of more than half the victims. The media had missed this fact, and the town had not received any crisis assistance at all, so we were able to be of use. After talking to the town's mayor, we were asked to speak to children during school time, as well as work with the community, creating a crisis counseling center in a local church. I've never forgotten the lesson. And in New York, I was impressed again with what experience had taught us. Being willing to go is only the beginning. Waiting is also serving. And sometimes studied listening, watching for doors to open, is another word for prayer.

That Sunday afternoon, we decided to return to Staten Island to attend the city's first memorial service being simulcast from Yankee Stadium to Staten Island's baseball farm team stadium. The small stadium was about half full for the four-hour service. Even though the effort was a good attempt, I could tell that it was being held way too early. I didn't see a lot of peace or comfort in the faces surrounding me. What we probably learned is that for a catastrophic event of this nature, people cannot be rushed. Memorializing victims is hard when so many bodies had yet to be found, so many lives yet to be officially pronounced at an end. Denial was still strong.

Part of the problem, I believe, was that the families had yet to be allowed into the site. That would soon change, and it would be the first step toward the resolution everyone wanted so desperately.

As we left Staten Island, Homeport and its marvelous volunteers stayed in my mind. The volunteer dynamic was a wonder to watch at any tragedy, but the uniquely American quality of the volunteerism here was what amazed me—it was as immense as the disaster itself. There was one aspect of this disaster, however, that was different from any crisis event we had faced: New Yorkers had spiritualized this event. As I moved through the city, I had been impressed with this fact beyond any other—people were so open to God, some for the first time, even if only through their rage. "I hate you!" a young woman had yelled at me one day as I walked by her. "I hate all you and all that your religions stand for!"

Be it good, bad, or ugly, every conversation included spiritual dialogue—on the subway, along the ground zero site perimeter, in the relief centers, on the sidewalks, on the ferry, in the moonlight and in the dust-filled sunshine. It flowed naturally and urgently.

Recent American disaster experiences, such as Oklahoma City's federal-building attack, the spate of schoolyard shootings, and the first World Trade Center bombing, all made us wonder about evil, yet not to the point of deep spiritual reflection. School and restaurant shootings were about madness and cultural problems. The Oklahoma City domestic terrorist bombing was seen as a criminal act, and Timothy McVeigh was executed for it. Evil it was, no doubt; misguided it was, without question. But no one demanded to know its deep spiritual implications.

But something beyond imagination had happened for New Yorkers, and it had happened on an incredible scale. That the Twin Towers were destroyed, and destroyed so completely, was beyond physical comprehension. It had already been tried and had failed. On February 23, 1993, six people were killed and a thousand injured when Islamic extremists detonated bombs in a parking garage beneath the towers. But the buildings had held, and that only reinforced the idea of their invincibility. I remember a moment in Oklahoma City after meeting the men who had been the primary emergency squad at the World Trade Center bombing—the NY-USAR team. They were the undeniable experts of this new field. As we were discussing the bombing, one of the squad members had commented, "Those buildings will never come down. It's impossible." The rest of the squad had agreed without a sliver of doubt.

When the impossible happens, a supernatural reason is needed. For the Western mind-set, a supernatural reason is a spiritual one. So the hunger for a spiritual answer to this event was insatiable: *Is this how it all ends? Tell me the spiritual implications. Answer my questions. Talk to me, Chaplain.* Questions were in the air as much as the towers' dust, be they angry, anxious, fearful, or sad. I had seen nothing like it in all my years of crisis work.

And as New York City was searching, so was the rest of America. That had been obvious from my first steps into the Las Vegas airport. In the weeks ahead, much would be written in the nation's press about a "Great Awakening" throughout the country. What did that say for us all? Can we doubt we are spiritual beings, no matter how we express it or attempt to suppress it?

New Yorkers responded by filling the city's church pews. "God in the Ruins?" asked a *New York* magazine's front-page headline. Inside, "Deliver Us from Evil" was the name of the article exploring the spiritual quest happening in the most cosmopolitan of all world cities. That this attack was an act of incredible evil seemed to go without saying. The nature of evil on this level was inspiring as many questions as the nature of God. Any discussion of evil had to include one about good. And if the good be God, then where was God? I kept thinking of it all in the words of Homeport's Ronnie: Was God "in the house"?

In the earliest days, the answers most heard were the extremes. On one end were those calling it the judgment of God for the sins of our nation. On the other end were those who believed it nothing more than a physical phenomenon—hijacked planes had hit the buildings, causing a fire that burned so hot the buildings' steel framing melted, and they collapsed, killing the people still in them. It didn't mean anything.

Both extremes were dismissed quickly. The former sounded far too similar to the fanatical religious view that created the crisis. As one New York pastor put it in print, "I say as lovingly as I can, it's bad theology." The latter seemed also incomprehensible, pointing to life without meaning of any kind. The human condition demanded more.

As the autumn's anthrax scare began and rumors of more attacks spread, the questioning multiplied. The nation's pews were filled; pastors and priests and rabbis were being challenged as never before to make faith relevant. Some would rise to the occasion; some would not. People were wanting more than pat answers to their questions, and many of the responses weren't satisfying the searchers. The tension was as old as the story of Job.

Most people also had little patience for hearing the right answers at the wrong time. In the earliest days, what was needed most was the one true answer we already had, the clearest one God had ever given—to love your neighbor. One Episcopal priest's experience on the first Sunday following the event encapsulated that feeling. Anticipating the large crowd that would attend, he had labored over how best to deliver the "right" political and ethical response to the tragedy. Afterward a parishioner came up to him, tears in her eyes, and said, "Father, all we wanted you to do was put your arms around us."

The demand for a personal spiritual response to this attack was so great that I began to realize people would find answers one way or another, with or without help. I wondered if the country's much-discussed Great Awakening might finally be, really, a quiet awakening in one heart at a time. I recall a survivor's letter printed in *USA Today* that ended with the changes the woman had made in her life. One change was valuing every day, another change was ending a bad relationship, and yet another was joining a church in a quest to find the purpose for living. And then she wrote of a monumental change of "awakening" proportions in any life: She now understood the "power of prayer," as she put it. "Not a day goes by," she wrote, "without a conversation with God."

For better or worse, though, the terrorist attack had created a spiritual crisis as well as an emotional and physical one, and it had spilled out onto the streets. The presence of Bibles everywhere I looked was proof of that. People would all but wave Bibles at me, especially the pocket-sized Gideon Bibles being given away throughout the area. During a rest break while digging on the pile one night, an ESU (emergency service unit) police officer pulled one of the small Bibles from his fatigues and showed it to me. "You know, years ago they tried to give out these books at the stations, but none of us would take them. And look at us now."

My team members and I began to carry a few with us to offer when asked. But we were surprised at the overwhelming demand. One of those early rainy nights, so wet that even the ironworkers were forced to take a long break, we were talking with a group of them while hunkered down in one of the damaged buildings. Window glass was falling around us, but we were out of the wind and rain and other falling debris, if you could imagine the irony of that. Here we were in a broken-down building that was the safest place we could be. The chaplain with me pulled a few candy bars from her bag to offer to the burly men. "Want some candy?" she asked one of the men. To get to them, she had to pull out the stashed pocket Bibles.

"No, but I'll take one of those."

"What?" she asked.

"Those," he repeated, pointing to the small Bibles still in her other hand.

"Me, too," said another. And another.

In a few seconds, the crew had cleaned our pockets of the little Bibles.

A few days later, two of us were rushing through the subway when we heard someone singing. In one of the passageways, an African-American woman stood singing a gospel song. A crowd had gathered, growing larger the longer she sang. Fifty or sixty people had gathered to bask in the comfort of her big voice and the song. She had no tip jar or hat set out, no church literature piled nearby; it wasn't about that. She was only offering what she had to give. I wanted to hug her for what she was doing for us. Only a few minutes earlier, we had stuffed some of the small Gideon Bibles in our fanny packs. My team member held up one of the little Bibles so the woman, as she sung, could see it. She gave us a quick nod, and we laid them all at her feet. As quickly as we laid them down, they were gone. It was as if people were saying, *Give me something that will bring me peace, words to read, words of life.* I shouldn't have been surprised. The Bible has done that for centuries; after all, it is a collection of books written for people in crisis.

After one extremely tiring shift, I was leaving ground zero at

4:30 A.M. A whole group of volunteer chaplains were with me as we entered a subway station on our way back to our rooms. We were all barely able to trudge up to the turnstiles, we were so exhausted. As I had done dozens of times by that point, I held up our ground zero badges and waited to be waved through. The woman inside the subway booth, however, didn't even look up. "You gotta pay," she called at us through the little window.

My initial thought was, *Hey, lady, we're tired. We're dirty. It's 4:30 in the morning, and we all gotta pay? Give me a break.*

Instead I went over to her booth. She continued to ignore me; she still wouldn't look up. Now I was mad. That's when I noticed what she had her nose buried in; it was one of the pocket Gideon Bibles. My heart melted. She was so engrossed in the Scriptures, she hadn't even noticed who we were, what we were wearing, and where we'd been.

The only thing I could say to her was, "Are you enjoying it?"

She finally looked at me. She was startled. "Oh, oh, okay, go on through."

We passed through, but I kept thinking about her all the way down to the platform. So I left the other chaplains there and went back to talk to the woman. We chatted for a few minutes about the World Trade Center and about what she was reading. And as I left to finally catch the train, I encouraged her to keep on reading her little Gideon Bible.

Spiritual conversations on the street or in the subway were one thing; on the pile, they were something very different. They were more intense, of course, but often they went beyond words.

The work itself became an answer. I knew that, and so did almost everyone else in the city. As a priest named Tom Synan expressed it so eloquently in *New York* magazine: "The work that's going on now at ground zero, there's the work of God. People of every faith, tradition, you name it, all working together for the greater good. The brilliant evil has since been met and it's being overcome now by the greater power of love."

It's hard to describe how that evil could just suck the life out of you after days of being surrounded by it on the pile. But the workers continued to push past that obstacle, continuing to find that greater power. And frankly, I was humbled by their expressions of it. To watch how those working in the debris pile found answers on their own, as they had done with "God's House," was truly a sight beyond words. Even reporters were amazed. "What do you make of 'God's House'?" a *New York Daily News* reporter asked me one day.

What did I think of it? I thought it was amazing—the whole thing—that a few ruined building's beams would be left standing in the shape of crosses, that construction workers would find them and preserve them, and that hundreds of others would find comfort in seeing them. Here in the midst of all this destruction, the symbolic meaning of the cross could not have been more powerful. Think about it. The cross as a symbol of anything but death is a tiny miracle itself. Historically, until Jesus Christ lived and died, it stood only for one of the most torturous, inhuman executions devised by humanity. It could even have been a symbol for the evil horrors that created this place, a fitting symbol for horrific death. Instead, over the centuries, it became a sign of hope and healing because of the way the story of Christ ends—not with death but with life. It should be one of the most negative symbols imaginable; instead it is the most positive one conceivable.

With "God's House," the ground zero workers seemed to grasp a spiritual answer beyond words. A photographer captured this spiritual component embraced so naturally by those who faced the horror every day. And we were there.

On October 4, as my team members and I were walking into the ground zero area through the West Highway checkpoint, I noticed something being lowered from the ruined U.S. Customs Building, the site of "God's House," which was now being slowly razed. Construction workers were working on one of the steel-girder crosses from "God's House" as if it were a priceless work of art. As the cross was set into place to stand sentry over the pile, a priest in a robe, Bible in hand, approached it. We moved closer in time to be a part of the blessing of the cross by Father Brian Jordan, a friend of the late New York Fire Department chaplain Father Mychal Judge. That moment became one of the most famous photos of the disaster. That steel-beam cross would remain there for the entire length of the ground zero work.

CHAPTER**SEVEN**

End of Watch

September 24, 2001

. . . Where are all the people?

Last night someone asked me what the hardest part of ground zero is for me. Aside from the loss of significant innocent lives, the hardest part is that the buildings won't give us back our loved ones. Thousands perished, yet these fathers, mothers, husbands, wives, sons, and daughters have not been found dead or alive. The workers' prayer is to be able to find something to offer their families closure.

IN THE WEEK THAT FOLLOWED, we fell into a routine of sorts centered around working C-watch, the late-night shift. During the day, we'd begun counseling students, staff, and faculty at the community college near the site. In between, we tried to rest. Ground zero work was still slow for all shifts, especially C-watch. It had rained most nights, making the work slower. Most of the rescue effort focused on the stairwells. Workers believed that was where they would find survivors. So expectations were always high once a stairwell was unearthed. For the last couple of nights, the work had centered on one stairwell. The heavy equipment was pulling out big riveted portions of the stairwell. You could see the forms of the stairs. They were being lifted out in sections, but nothing could happen fast enough. So the work had become a doubly painful process. The frustration was not only being felt by the human rescuers. Some of the dogs had been trained specifically to find survivors. One of the handlers, I was told, had become so concerned about his dog that he had actually asked volunteers to hide under a blanket so his dog could finish a shift by "rescuing" a person.

Where were the people?

That was the unspoken question hanging in the air.

We came early Tuesday night, almost two weeks after arriving in New York. It was 10:30; shift change wasn't until 11. As we came on site, we passed a weary rescue worker who had been there since morning. "We're finding them," he said, pausing before he left. "We've been finding them most of the shift."

From the sound of his voice, I knew he was referring to bodies, not survivors. I turned to my team members, who had never experienced what I felt to be the most compelling reason for a chaplain's presence on a disaster site. "Tonight, it's going to really change," I said.

Our work at ground zero, to that point, had been for the living. It began as "Will you listen to us?" It became "Will you come in with us?" It turned into "Will you help us find the victims?" Now it would be "Will you help us honor our recovered brothers?"

I noticed only one other chaplain already on site, a priest

volunteer from a nearby church. As it would turn out, I would be the only one that night who knew the protocol. I picked up a body bag and an American flag at the command post, in anticipation, and headed deep into the pile. The farther I went, the worse the heat became. It was blistering and stinking, smoke pouring out as I went farther in. Everyone I saw looked wasted, drenched in his own sweat, drained from finding so many so fast.

Firefighters have a term for dying in service. They call it "end of watch." Whenever the body of a firefighter or police officer was discovered, work in the entire area stopped and everyone came to attention. Eight firefighters had already been found in this one stairwell. The site was too quiet. It was clear that another had just been uncovered.

"Chaplain," I heard a voice calling, "we got one here." It was a battalion chief covered from head to toe with the pile's dust, standing near the stairwell.

"Okay, chief, what do you want to do?" I said.

They had identified him from his ID label stitched inside his coat. "We want to get the company here," he answered. When a firefighter dies in the line of duty, his or her company is notified. If they are not on the scene, the firehouse is called and everyone waits until the company members arrive. This firefighter's own crew would be the ones who would honor him by carrying him off the hill.

"Okay, then this is the way we'll do it," I said. "Once we get him out of the stairwell, we'll cover him, and we'll have a prayer for him, his crew, and his family."

The firefighter's body was intact, and the gentleness the firefighters used in their attempts to keep the body that way while it was placed into the bag was heart-wrenching.

Although the smell was overpowering, no one wore a respirator mask. At first it appeared that the firefighters had taken them off in order to communicate better, but soon it was obvious that each man had taken off his mask as a sign of respect: *He's one of ours; he does not smell.*

The bagged remains were carefully placed in the Stokes basket as the site was fixed on a GPS global device, marking by satellite the exact time and place where he was recovered.

Because the recovered person had been a member of the emergency service, fire, or police—this man was a firefighter—a flag was to be used as part of the ritual. That's why I had brought one onto the pile with me. I had never seen the American flag used in quite the way it was used at ground zero. I had often seen it draped or set upon a casket. Here, however, the flag was placed on the body bag, its edges pressed into the sides of the Stokes basket that would be hoisted by his comrades. I would see this use over and over in the weeks ahead.

No members of the firefighter's company were on site, the battalion chief was told. He turned to me and said, "We've made the call." A senior fire chief had phoned the man's firehouse to inform the firefighters that one of their own had been found. "They are on the way."

"Well, we'll just wait, Chief. We've got him," I said. "And I'll stay with him." For the time it took the crew to come to the site, I stood as a sentry over the body, American flag in my arms, giving the battalion chief and the other firefighters and rescue workers permission to take care of other concerns, including each other's grief.

In a few minutes, the crew arrived.

Construction workers had moved the big boom above where we stood, their way of offering to carry down the body to street level, easily and quickly.

"No," responded one of the crew to the gesture. "We want to carry him off the hill." For this fire squad, participating in this man's ritual was the highest of honors. Bringing home one of their own from "end of watch" was the most intimate, most personal act of fire service they would ever perform.

After the firefighter's remains had been placed in the carrier and the flag had been placed around him, I said a prayer while his brothers- and sisters-in-service bowed their heads to show reverence.

Then workers from all over the site stopped their work, got off their rigs, removed their hats, and formed lines on both sides of the path that the firefighter's crew would take to carry his body off the pile.

A voice called out, "Lead us, Chaplain."

As I turned, we faced the others watching respectfully from a distance. As we proceeded carefully down the pile, we passed the halted machinery and the hundreds of workers who lined the path to the temporary morgue prepared at ground zero.

Midway through the descent, we paused again for another prayer, this one for the men who had found him.

We continued our walk, descending a good fifteen stories off the pile, stopping only once to allow the crew to reposition their hands carrying the sacred cargo.

At the temporary morgue set up near one of the command posts, we were greeted by those officials whose mission was to prepare the documentation that positively identified the deceased. They asked a few private questions of those who knew him well, and the ID was made. The firefighter had been Catholic. A priest assigned to the morgue was asked to bless the remains. We stepped back as the priest moved near to administer the sacrament.

Then we waited—all of us—until the New York Fire Department ambulance arrived. Leaving the temporary morgue, we saw a new group of workers standing five and six deep in formation. Police officers and National Guard members from the perimeter had come to pay a final respect.

The command was given.

Attention!

Immediately, those assembled saluted this fallen comrade as his crew placed him in the FDNY ambulance. Once loaded, solemnly and gently, the doors were closed, the driver and his aide climbed into the vehicle, the red lights were turned on, and the vehicle quietly rolled away. Everyone remained at full attention until the ambulance was gone. Then we returned to the work.

This happened many times during my C-watch work, sometimes involving two bodies at the same time in those early weeks. On that specific day, however, they had already found eight firefighters, so by the time I arrived, there already had been eight processions off the pile.

Before the night was over, I would do four more. And then, as quickly as the building had become merciful enough to give back bodies, it stopped once again.

October 2, 2001
. . . "Where are the people?"

During C-watch, we were given a dozen answers. For twelve fire-fighters, tonight was end of watch.

CHAPTER**EIGHT**

Fireman's Foster Child

October 2, 2001/October 16, 1961

. . . Life goes on, even after other lives end. Yet to be standing on the edge of life and death makes everyday issues crystal clear.

W E LIVE LIKE WE'RE SUPERMEN, running into buildings, standing on a pile of twisted steel as high as a skyscraper. If we ever stopped to meditate upon what we were doing, we could never do it: I'm standing in the air on a surface above a massive fire that is so unstable only one shift of the girders could make me fall into a void below.

And yet standing there on the edge of life and death, it was impossible not to think about life very clearly: *What's really important? What do I want? What should I do with the rest of my life? What kind of relationship should I have with my family, my spouse, my kids, all the people I love?*

And so I found myself talking about the most intimate things with these men, hovering there over the sixteen-hundred-degree heat. The pressures and decisions of everyday life didn't stop for the workers at ground zero. They still had the same mortgage payments, the same personal and financial obligations, and the same family concerns as they had before September 11. Life goes on. As we worked the remainder of that night and the ones that followed with little to show for it, we stopped, rested, and chatted in order to gain strength to keep going. And in those moments, the firefighters would talk about their families.

I was working with a small crew in a pit area behind the stairwell area. It was hot, and the machinery was moving around us. We took off our masks, and I struck up a conversation with the fireman standing by me.

"This doesn't get any easier," I said.

"No," he agreed. But then he shook his head. "I'm here digging, but this is nothing compared to what I face when I go home." And suddenly this firefighter was telling me about his family. He was a foster parent of two children, a four-year-old girl and a three-year-old boy. In less than a month, he and his wife had to make the decision whether to keep these children permanently or whether to let them go back into the system. The boy had been emotionally abused, severely, before coming under the firefighter's care, and he was having lots of problems. "And they're bad," the firefighter said, so bad he was deeply worried that the boy would wind up in prison. "I just love him so much; I love both of them so much," he admitted. "But I don't know if I have what it takes to become their father."

I took a deep breath. Of all the chaplains who could have been at ground zero that night, of all the fellow workers to whom he could have mentioned this situation, he was standing next to a man who had been a foster child. So I began to help him talk through the situation. God had given him the responsibility for that young boy's life today, I assured him, not fifteen years from now. Only today was his to mold, and the days ahead could be just as affected by love as the boy's yesterdays were affected by anger.

But what I wasn't saying was perhaps much more persuasive. A special mixture of such days was the reason I was standing there with him. The fact is—I'm a living miracle of a chain of events, a family drama, that could just as easily have led me to prison instead of there, at ground zero, talking to him.

And so I said, "I need to tell you a story."

I HAD ALWAYS KNOWN I had another name. I was born Raymond Thomas Lanigan in Trenton, New Jersey, to an Irish Catholic father and an Italian Catholic mother. I was the last of nine children born in ten years. My mother had a child every year, except for one year in which she miscarried. In 1960, the year I was born, my father began serving a sentence in the New Jersey State Prison. So my young mother was left to raise nine children, five boys and four girls, entirely alone. One day, when I was ten months old, she went out for bread and never came home.

My mother had told my ten-year-old sister to watch all of us while she went to the market. As the hours turned into days, my oldest sister moved me to the second floor of the ramshackle frame house in which the state welfare bureau had placed us. To keep me out of harm's way, my sister laid me in an open bureau drawer, the closest thing to a crib we had. As the days went by, she fed us kids with whatever food was left in the house, until it was all gone.

Finally, at the end of a week, she went next-door to ask the neighbors if they had seen our mother, still believing she would return. She believed this because my mother had been missing before; the last time, several months earlier, she had returned in three days. The neighbors immediately alerted the police, who were already familiar with the dire conditions of our family situation. My father, a long-haul truckdriver, was serving a one-year prison term for failure to support his family, after years of neglect due to his drinking. So we had been abandoned, in reality, by both parents.

That day we were all separated, my brothers and sisters put into foster homes and my youngest sister and I hospitalized due to malnutrition, dehydration, and infected sores from the neglect. I was later told my skin was peeling off, I was so near death. My mother had a brother and a sister, and my father had seven siblings, but our extended family did not take any of us.

My father would die four years later of cirrhosis of the liver. My mother was never found.

As I mentioned earlier, I wouldn't know a word of this story for another quarter-century. I was not even aware I had brothers and sisters until 1986. Catholic charities had taken me directly from the hospital as a baby and placed me in foster care with a family named Giunta who were fostering several other children, along with raising their own daughter. They had not been told any of the details of my birth family's saga, either. My foster father and mother were quite loving to their foster children, unlike the grim stories some of my siblings would later tell of their own foster experiences, in which they were treated as little more than free child labor.

When I was four years old, the Giuntas decided to stop their foster-care work. All the other foster children had places to go but me. One of my earliest memories is of being asked by my foster father and mother whether I'd like to live there permanently. I said yes, please, I would. After all, it was the only home I had ever known, and they were the only parents I had ever really had. At the adoption proceedings, I stood on one of the courtroom tables and answered yes again to the same question. I recall a celebration that day almost like a birthday, which it was, in a way—a re-birthday. On that day I became a Giunta and acquired all that went along with being a member of the family. As it turned out, that included an extremely different future than that experienced by my birth siblings. My adopted father was in the military, and soon we had moved halfway around the world. I spent the remainder of my childhood in Germany and Italy, attaining a fine education and enjoying the privilege of growing up amid other cultures. After graduating from high school, I came back to the States, went to college, and got married.

Then one day in 1986, Raymond Giunta would find out about Raymond Lanigan. And the discovery would make national news.

As my wife, Cathy, and I planned for the arrival of our first child, she asked me what I knew of my family. Her doctor was asking questions about our medical histories. I told her I knew nothing more than my birth surname and my birthplace. I didn't want to admit, even to myself, that I had the typical adopted child's natural reservations about the personal unknown. I had dreamed as a child of my real parents, of their glorious and dramatic deaths, creating fancy adventures to substitute for the very large gaps in my real story. The fact is, though, I never imagined there was anything more to know about my past beyond my birth parents' names and my birthplace, since that was all my adoptive parents knew. I had no idea what had happened to us or even that there was an "us."

"Let's leave it alone," I told my wife.

But my wife was insistent. At the time, I was a criminal investigator for the state of California, so she knew if there was history to be found I could certainly find it. Of course, I knew that such searches often did not end well or successfully; laws existed for that very purpose. And we both knew I couldn't, and shouldn't, break any laws to find the information. Finally I agreed to make an attempt for the sake of my first child, Kimberlee. And that one small attempt set into motion a chain of events that led me back to my own truth. My history, my brand-new past, unfolded as if it were waiting for me. It was almost breathtaking in its simplicity.

Since I knew my birth surname, I went to a nearby university library and researched microfiche of old New Jersey phone books. In the 1960 Trenton phone book, I found three Lanigans listed. I picked up the phone and dialed.

In hindsight, I admit that sounds strange. What were the odds that someone would have the same phone number after twenty-five years? But that didn't seem to occur to me at the time. I called the first number; it was disconnected. I called the second one; no response. When I dialed the third phone number, a man answered.

"Yes, our name is Lanigan," he said.

"Can you tell me the history of the Lanigans in Trenton?" I asked the man. "Do you remember a time when someone might have been killed or died in the family, and maybe a child was born during it all? I'm a Lanigan, and I'm trying to find out if I'm part of your family."

The man was abrupt. "I don't know. My father might. This is his house. He's been in this town for years, but he's in Florida right now vacationing. If he knows anything, I'll give him your number, and he'll call you."

With that, I let it go. I told my wife that the phone call was all I could do, that I really did not want to violate the law by attempting to see sealed records.

A few weeks later, I was sitting at home on a Saturday afternoon watching the New York Mets play the San Francisco Giants in preseason when the phone rang. I will never forget the time: 4:00 P.M. A woman on the other end of the phone began to ask me question after question. Was my name Raymond Lanigan? Was I born in New Jersey? Had I ever lived in Trenton? Was I born in 1960?

Finally I stopped her and asked, "What's this about? Why are you calling?"

The voice on the other end of the phone went silent. After a few seconds, I could hear the woman begin to cry. "We've looked for you for twenty-five years, and we have finally found you," she said. The woman was my sister.

She began to tell me the entire story. Consider how strange it would all sound upon hearing it for the first time.

"How many have you found?" I asked when I finally recovered my voice.

"Five of us, the oldest five. Most of us were able to stay in touch through the years," she answered.

"But what's the status of the others?"

"We don't know. You're the sixth, and there are still three left," she said. Two of the younger brothers were still "missing," as was my youngest sister. "But now that we've found you, we want to have a reunion," she said. "Can you come to New Jersey?"

I could, and I did. During Easter week of 1986, I met my brothers and sisters. I was amazed at how much we resembled each other, as probably any "orphan" might be upon first seeing his family. Of course, the fact of this whole, new personal history was remarkable for me, but for my siblings, there was nothing new or remarkable about it at all. These women and men, my older sisters and brothers, were old enough to remember my parents, to remember being separated from each other, and to wonder what happened to their mother and the baby brother they had cared for. For them, the last quarter-century had been deeply painful, a wound that had never healed. They knew what they had lost; I didn't know. But once I found out, I was never the same.

And now, I wanted to know everything.

My brothers and sisters, however, didn't know much more than what I had already been told. They were able to take me to my father's grave. They also believed they knew where our mother's sister might live, although they had never found the courage to approach her, the pain being too much to face. But I talked my brand-new sibling clan into going to see this aunt of ours, in hopes of collecting more pieces of our collective story. In fact, I began to believe that it might be possible to find us all, and not only that, to find them *now.*

So that week, after waiting twenty-five years, six of us began a journey to find all nine of us.

We knocked on our aunt's door and waited in silent anticipation. We were about to meet a member of our mother's family. I couldn't help but wonder if my mother had once stood at this very spot. A fair-skinned woman in her sixties opened the door, and we all introduced ourselves to our Aunt Rose. She could have slammed the door on us, keeping what had to be an equally painful part of her past closed forever. Instead, she invited us in and told us what she recalled of that day long ago. Then she paused and told us one thing more. Years before, she was certain she had seen our mother in the Irish area of Upper Manhattan, living on the streets. But when our aunt approached the homeless woman, the woman had answered, "I don't have a family, I don't have any children, and I don't know you."

We never knew whether that story was something my aunt, with her own trials, had to believe to survive or whether there was any validity to her sighting. But Aunt Rose was certain that the homeless person was my mother, her lost sister. And anything seemed possible that week. So the next day, despite the intervening years and the odds against that homeless woman being our mother, we actually traveled to that specific Manhattan area on the off chance that we might see the woman ourselves.

We didn't, of course, but instead of being discouraged, we went home, turned on the television, and watched the next installment of our family reunion miracle unfold.

By that time, we had already been the subjects of numerous features in newspapers as well as local television news, both in California and New Jersey. My wife, a third-grade teacher, had told her students about my sibling discovery. One of the students' parents had contacted the local media about it, and within a matter of days, the story had attracted not only local but national interest. Soon our saga became a national human-interest story on NBC News—and, amazingly enough, it aired during the week of my visit in Trenton.

This was not the first time we had made the news. Immediately after my sister told me our story, I had done more research, this time in historical archives of New Jersey newspapers, circa 1961. We had first made front-page headlines on the day after we were found abandoned. The story had been covered heavily. "MOTHER HUNTED FOR DESERTION OF 9 KIDS," the headline read.

In 1961, that coverage had not found our mother or helped us in any tangible way. But the timing of this new media exposure, the national NBC television news story, would become a surprising part of the rest of our search. It would produce two little miracles of human kindness for our Lanigan reunion.

The first came within a few hours of the television feature's airing. The phone rang at my sister's home, where I was staying. The woman on the other end introduced herself. "I'm the social worker who handled the case twenty-five years ago," she said. "I handled the adoption of your brother that you just found, but I also handled the adoption of your sister. Have you found her yet?"

No, we hadn't, my sister told her.

The social worker explained that she had worked hard to keep the babies together, my two-year-old sister and myself, trying to find someone who would take two infants. She hadn't been successful, though, and it had always bothered her. Now, all these years later, she was extremely glad for another chance to help. "I can't give you the information," the social worker added, "but this is what I can do. I know her number, so I'll call her. If she's interested in getting hold of you, she can."

Very soon, the phone rang again, and on the other end of the line was our missing baby sister. She had lived in Trenton her entire life, adopted by a family only a few miles from where we sat.

So, incredibly, within a matter of hours, my youngest sister appeared at my eldest sister's door. As she came in, my sister ran up to her. But instead of hugging her, my eldest sister first reached for her right hand. She looked closely at a prominent scar on the hand then began to openly weep for joy. "I remember when you put your hand through the wringer of our washer. I told Mom that your hand needed attention, and she didn't take care of it. I always knew that if I ever saw you again, it would be scarred."

We Lanigans were now up to seven. We had only two more brothers left to find. Figuring that they had, like the other Lanigans, stayed in New Jersey, we went, en masse, to the nearest Department of Motor Vehicles office, hoping against hope that the officials might give us the information. The woman at the DMV counter we approached was abrupt.

"Are you the kid from California who just found your family?" she asked me, looking me up and down.

"Yes, I am," I answered.

"Go down to the end of the counter and wait for me." So we paraded over there and waited.

Finally the woman appeared again, and this time she was anything but abrupt. "I saw you on television. I could lose my job for this, but the story has so moved me, it would be worth it. Here's the address of your brother. He lives in New Brunswick."

After a heartfelt thank you, we drove to New Brunswick, New Jersey, and showed up on my brother's doorstep. We Lanigans, all looking very much alike, waited for the door to open. When it did, a woman stood there with a dark-haired little boy who also looked very much like us. She was our brother's wife. And after she heard our story, she picked up her phone and called her husband at work. He immediately came home to a house full of new family.

That left one more brother to find.

"I know where he is," my latest brother said. As they grew up in orphanages, foster care, and reform schools, they, at least, had been able to keep up with each other. So, on Sunday, the day before I was to fly home, eight of the nine long-lost Lanigans had one last reunion get-together at a restaurant. And in walked the last brother to make the reunion complete.

After a quarter-century, the Lanigan siblings were reunited on Easter Sunday, 1986.

For a very long time, I didn't quite know what to make of this story. That it was my sudden, new life story only made it harder for me to wrap my mind around it. I couldn't shake the feeling that it meant something beyond an overwhelmed woman losing the grip on her wits, and the fallout it created in nine lives. It's one thing to go through life grateful that a compassionate family came along to take care of you after your parents had died; it's another to hear you should have died and would have except for the care of a ten-year old sister you did not even know you had. Life had been hard for my siblings. The pain was reflected on all these new, familiar faces I saw as they told their stories. Each story could have been mine; each face could have been mine.

People talk about visions and callings and such. For me, the major turning point in my life was this new reality—discovering I had a family from another existence, that nothing about myself was as I believed, and that out of nothing but mercy I had landed safely in a whole other life. When such mercy happens to you over the course of a lifetime, it may seem more the result of fortitude or good judgment. When such mercy is revealed suddenly, it's as if you see yourself—how you came to be who you are—

rolled out for inspection. The hand of providence is hard to refute. It might take years to process it all, but you know one thing beyond doubt—you were handed a gift.

And so, just as the survivors of September 11 have done with their own stories of mercy, I looked for meaning in mine. As much as I loved having found my biological family, I lived three thousand miles and twenty-five years away from them. This reunion miracle had to be about more than having a sudden web of family ties. As wonderful as these people were, we could not recover what we never had. We all have roles to play while on this planet, complete with the individual obstacles of any full life. Theirs was to carry that story with them while tackling their personal hurdles. What was mine? I wanted to know. In my own life, I had failed so many times and in so many ways. Yet if God had protected me all those years, he must have wanted me to do more with my life than prosecuting people for committing forgery.

I was overwhelmed for a very long time; I remember a real stirring in my spirit over the events and the revelations of that amazing Easter week. And I recall even then attributing it all to God; no part of it did I call coincidence. I experienced a kind of cataclysmic awakening, suddenly realizing there was more to life than just me. In my family's story of tragedy and restoration, I experienced the first act of dramatic redemption I had ever known. I was a Christian and a church member, and I truly believed and had accepted the gift of a personal God through Christ. It was all valid and true, and had been for years. But I tend to believe that we human beings don't truly understand grace until we've been on the powerful receiving end of it. That reunion miracle was the first time I recognized the grace of God in action. Not until that moment had I understood the depth of God's love. Suddenly, being a Christian took on a brand-new meaning. That God could take something that was so broken and put it all back together so dramatically and so quickly was proof-positive, for me, of divine love and all its powerful possibilities.

Since my days at a Jesuit high school in Rome, I'd flirted with ministry. The priesthood had held promise—until I discovered girls. I had gone into law enforcement as another way to help people, but I only came in contact with those I was sending to jail, and their stories rarely ended well. I'd investigate my cases, I'd write the reports, I'd pick up the pieces, and I'd go home to start all over the next day, working to jail people who had little hope for the future. After that Easter weekend in New Jersey, though, I no longer saw dead-ends for the daily human crises surrounding me; I saw the possibility of resolution. I saw hope for humanity, just as I saw a new kind of hope for my own life. I found myself slipping small amounts of money to those I helped convict, saying, "Here. Take care of your family. Don't steal." After a while, I understood that what I was really doing was giving my father money to help feed *his* family. That's when I realized I'd better get out of law enforcement before I got hurt or before I got some-body else hurt. So, after talking it over with my wife, I quit my detective job, even though I now had a family myself. Yet I never worried. How could I? Anything seemed possible now, and noth-ing seemed impossible.

I went back to school, this time for a theological degree. But I didn't go to Bible college to become a minister. I went to Bible college to learn the Bible. I wanted to grow up in my faith. Christ was becoming more clear to me, more real to me. I let that happen. My call to ministry was really more of a process that began after my miracle Easter week in New Jersey. I began to do volunteer work at the church, being an usher and such things, as I studied. Finally, when I finished the degree, it was in pastoral studies, and I was ready to start a new career as a minister, ready to see what God had in mind for me.

Very quickly, though, I realized the traditional congregational role of a minister neither satisfied me nor suited whatever gifts I had to offer. I hadn't left a government career, sold two BMWs, and lived on peanut butter and jelly sandwiches to referee church members' squabbles. I explored the hospital chaplaincy. But even there, I was always listening for the code calls to the emergency room. I wanted to be where people's needs were immediate and raw. That's what mattered to me, that people were hurting. I was convinced that's where Christ would be, with hurting people. I don't remember a day as a member of the clergy that I haven't looked for ways to help people in crisis.

So on that day in 1987 when I read a headline about two little boys who had been run over by a car, my empathy for their single mothers propelled me into my crisis-chaplaincy future. I had just read a stunning statistic: 70 percent of city dwellers, seven out of ten, did not have any affiliation to a local religious organization, the institutions that have always met humanity's basic life-and-death needs. Family also was no longer the traditional, immediate, safety net. Modern life fragmented our families through divorce and distance. Funeral homes had become less personalized as they had become big business. And funerals cost more than many people had, including the families of these two boys. *Who was helping these people?* I suddenly thought, knowing full well the limitations of governmental agencies. I knew our church wasn't sending anyone out there. So I told my secretary that I was going to find the boys' families.

"But how?" she asked.

With my law enforcement background, that was the easy part. Standing in the presence of two mourning mothers was much harder. I had walked past the yellow tape that police use to surround a crime scene and found the two women in the same apartment, weeping together.

"I'm here to help you and your sons any way I can," I said after I introduced myself. "Do you have a local pastor or priest to help you with proper burial arrangements?"

"No," they admitted.

"Do you have any plans at all for the boys?"

"We don't know what to do."

I did know, so I led them through the maze of arrangements as best I could. And from the scene of two small boys' deaths, a path has led through similar scenes at school shootings, earthquakes, bombings, and terrorist attacks—tragedies large and small, dealing with one grieving heart at a time. As I look back now, everything in my life seemed to have been leading to compassionate crisis work. A life begun in crisis became a life spent helping people in crisis—with a powerful personal story to share. I would be years understanding the unconscious process, but that discovery would propel me all the way to the World Trade Center's ground zero on that night in 2001 where a firefighter was worried about his foster children. It would be the catalyst in my life that would allow me to begin to say, "No problem" to whatever came. Knock on the door of a dead child's parent? "No problem." Travel to Oklahoma City? "No problem." Go to ground zero? "No problem." After what I experienced that Easter week in 1986, I understood that the impossible was child's play for God, and my life was no longer my own.

I have been asked what would I say to my mother if I met her. During those months working in Manhattan, I thought about her many times. One night while walking through the ground zero area, I saw some blankets and a grocery cart full of the kinds of things collected by a person living on the streets. "They must have belonged to a homeless person killed in the buildings' collapse," I commented to a fellow chaplain who knew my story. "For all I know, that could have been my mother."

Odds are it wasn't, of course; forty years is an impossibly long time to live on the streets of New York City. The odds, however, would have also been stacked against *my* being alive. And the odds would have been even higher that all nine of her children were still alive and that we would find each other. What would I say to my mother if we were reunited? I have thought quite a bit about that question. I wanted my heart to be ready for such a moment, even knowing the odds were a million to one it would ever happen. Either way, I wanted my heart to be at peace. So I know what I would say to her. If she had lived all this time, then she had lived with guilt and shame and worries enough for any life. Having been forgiven myself, how could I offer any less to her? So I always felt if I were allowed to meet her, it would be for one reason alone. It would be for God to say to her, through me, "It's okay, Mom. God took care of me."

I FINISHED TELLING MY STORY to the fireman foster dad. The other workers had already gone back to the digging. But he wanted to keep talking. His decision still had to be made, and there was no doubt he had the right listening ear. The decisions of everyday life, small choices as well as headline-creating ones, all affect someone, somehow, someday. The future is decided in such instances, for good or bad. And yet God's grace found in those blessed moments—in the wake of one phone call or on top of a twenty-story-tall disaster scene—can make all the difference.

That I was standing there at ground zero to tell my story to this foster-father fireman was all the testament to that truth either of us needed.

Chapter Nine

Fifth Wave

October 3, 2001

. . . Today a new reality level was grasped by most of us at ground zero. As the firemen sat in fresh, empty turnouts, you could see in their faces the sentiments echoed by a construction superintendent: "It is a demolition now." Four waves of belief had been felt over the course of just twenty-four days. First, the shock that something truly evil did happen—it was not a dream, and we were not going to wake up. Then came the belief that some died but many could still be found alive. After that came the belief that while there were no more survivors, the bodies would be recovered and returned to their families.

And now the new reality: The majority will not be found at all.

CRISIS WORKERS TALK in terms of "waves." In New York City, the first wave had been the disaster event itself. The planes hit, the buildings fell, and in the crucial first minutes after the collapse, many people were saved.

The second wave had been the rescue attempt. The planes hit, the buildings fell down, quite a few people died, but thousands could still be rescued.

Then we had moved into the third wave. There would be no more survivors. The rescue effort became a recovery mission. Massive numbers of people had been killed, but workers were still going to come to the site every day to help return bodies to the grieving families.

The acceptance was a somber one, but it soon settled over all of us at ground zero as the work continued.

October 3, 2001

. . . Spent most of night with ESU—a special police operation unit that lost fourteen men. We worked with them for many hours, sharing a meal, words of comfort, and a time of prayer at the makeshift memorial for their friends.

October 4, 2001

. . . Tonight it rained, and the job was very slow. Three weeks into this, and the cleanup is only at 15 percent. Pray for the craft workers' safety. The Teamsters, the ironworkers, the carpenters, and the operating engineers are unsung heroes with no official support systems. It is taking its toll.

On Tuesday night, we had stayed with the firefighters for the entire shift, finding so many of their colleagues and helping bring them home. The next night, however, we would spend with an ESU squad, the elite emergency service unit of the police department that basically does the same duty as a fire/rescue unit. As soon as we walked onto the site, they called to us, waving us over to where they stood by one of the off-road vehicles used to get around ground zero. The squad was dirty, head to toe. Typically, police officers are known for a certain kind of humor, which they use like a shield. And I had heard it in their voices as they called us over. So, seeing how dirty they were, I commented, "Been a busy night?"

In place of the banter I expected, one of them said, "Hey, chaplains, we got you tonight. Ride with us." Early in the night, they had uncovered the remains of two police officers, I was to find out. It was the first time since the attack that the remains of any police had been recovered. In a worst-case scenario, police officers can be identified by their weapons, handcuffs, or the badge number on the back of their belt buckles. And this discovery had been a worst-case scenario—the ESU officers were only able to identify their comrades through these small objects of their profession. After that, they didn't really want to go back to business as usual. Hanging around with some chaplains sounded right. Instead of our adopting them, they wanted to adopt us for the shift. So I took off my glove and headed toward these guys, my hand outstretched.

Touch is a large part of crisis work, often a surprisingly important one. Big, tough firefighters embrace each other freely in such a setting, bear hugs and a couple of pats on the back given out like good medicine. Emergency personnel of all kinds will stride right up and give each other a hug hello. Handshakes become as much about touch as they are about greeting, so it's important that gloves come off. Everybody wore gloves at ground zero, but no one shook hands with his or her gloves on. We were standing in a dirty and dangerous place where gloves were essential, yet every single handshake encounter was a gloves-off moment. After the first few days, unless I was literally digging in the pile, I rarely wore my right glove because I got tired of taking it off. That's how much crisis workers desire that physical touch, even, perhaps, without knowing it.

Sometimes we all get to that place where words aren't enough. Only a touch communicates. Many nights, because of the noise or the work in progress, all I could do was put a hand on a shoulder or touch an arm as I passed, in effect saying, "Nice job." But it made a difference. When I train volunteer chaplains, I spend a lot of time talking about the right and wrong approaches of touch during crisis work. There are right and wrong ways even to offer a handkerchief. When someone is crying, you can present a tissue in a way that all but tells the person he or she should not be crying. Or you can do it in a way that gives permission to cry. The same dynamic exists for a comforting light touch in crisis.

Perhaps what worried me the most for the construction workers on the site was their lack of opportunity for such unspoken communication. This was especially true for the members of the International Operating Engineers, Locals 14 and 15, who worked the heavy machines such as cranes, excavators, and front loaders—the "dwellers of the pit," as one reporter dubbed them—cutting and moving beams that allowed workers access into the voids. Inside their big rigs, no one could even give them a pat on the back.

On Thursday's shift, we had our first chance to talk with some of the Teamsters. The thousand-ton cranes I had seen being assembled on my first night at the World Trade Center site had now been reaching into the skies above the pile for more than a week. They were moving twenty-foot-by-twelve-foot blocks of the pile's mass in one motion, placing the material either on a flatbed truck or into a dump truck on its way to the Fresh Kills landfill. It was an amazing engineering feat to watch.

The teamwork among the civilian workers and the professional relief workers, all working side by side, was also a marvel. Firefighters, for instance, would allow these Teamsters to drop them into areas via the heavy equipment baskets. Rescue professionals were trusting their lives to these construction crews they had never met, without question. According to an article I recall reading in the *New York Times,* they had worked even more in tandem than I was aware of during a search for a door leading to a vault of gold bullion that was somewhere in the pile. The firefighters had directed the operators where to gingerly scoop and rake until the door to millions in dollars of stored gold bullion was uncovered. Meanwhile, engineers were also working underneath the damaged World Trade Center foundation to keep the Hudson River from flooding the portions of Lower Manhattan built on fill from the original Twin Towers construction.

Above us and below us now, these civilian workers were on the job as faithfully and intensely as the fire service or the police service. This was the first time civilian personnel have had to be used in such a massive way at a crime scene. In Oklahoma City, civilian machinery operators were used. But officials could see the underside of the building, knew the scope of the damage, and were able to minimize the danger they were in as well as the time they had to spend there.

The stress at the Manhattan disaster site, however, was taking an almost unseen toll on these guys. The civilian workers were the unsung heroes of the relief work, in my view. And they were probably the ground zero group with the highest risk for trauma issues. Many of these men were working twelve hours a day, seven days a week, and they would do it for so long that many of them would begin to call life beyond the pile, the "outside world." Unlike firefighters, they didn't have a company filled with colleagues to return to. They didn't have a squad they were working with all the time. They had never had any CISM (Critical Incident Stress Management) training. They were not trained to uncover body parts, much less know what to do about what they saw from their perch high above the work.

One of the first construction workers I met was a man named Tom. We talked for a moment during a rare break in his work. He was an operating engineer, a union classification for those who operate heavy pieces of machinery. The operating seat for the rig he worked, an excavator, was perched up high over the site, so as bodies and body remains were uncovered, he could see them all clearly, along with a full view of the activity each discovery generated. After three shifts in a row of finding bodies in the stairwells, Tom was almost to his breaking point.

I asked him how he was doing. He did not look good.

"Every time I make a cut," he admitted, "I worry that some-body is still alive back there. How do I know I'm not killing someone when I scoop?"

I assured him that cameras had searched the stairwell areas over and over again. Rescue workers also had gone in personally to search each place prior to his order to remove it.

"Yeah," he said, "but even if they're not alive, I'm still destroy-ing bodies. I'm ripping people apart, for God's sake," he gasped. "That's not my job."

After hearing several such comments from these men in the nights ahead, I suggested to one of the construction superintend-ents that we take an hour to make sure they're all okay. "We should make sure they're going home, that they're eating, drink-ing water, and resting properly so that when they return to operate these big pieces of equipment each day, they come back healthy, fresh, and safe," I explained.

"Oh no, they do this all the time," the superintendent answered.

"Who does this all the time?" I said. "Who has ever done *this* all the time?"

"No, I mean they demolish things. They're used to these long hours, seven days a week. They love it. They're getting big paychecks."

He didn't understand. And how could he? Neither he nor any of his "brothers" had ever been asked to add the stress of seeing death to the long hours they worked. No paycheck, I had to believe, was big enough to make that worthwhile without the support and coping skills available to relief professionals.

Occasionally I noticed a few of the construction workers doing their best to take care of themselves. Despite the time pressures they worked under, they'd battle the loneliness of their work by finding quick ways to connect with the rest of us. One night, as one of the volunteer chaplains and I were walking by, a crane operator opened his door and called down to us, "Hey, I got three Gummi Life Savers left. I figure you chaplains are the lifesavers down there, so you might like having 'em." And then he shared his three little pieces of candy, one for each of us, him included.

In the weeks and months ahead, these construction workers would feel the brunt of the work as the site became more and more a demolition site. A man named Andrew reminded me just what can happen when someone pushes himself too far, too long, without support.

Late in November, as I walked up to a checkpoint, a National Guard sergeant said, "We could use your help." To my left, National Guard and police officers stationed at the checkpoint were coping with what looked like a drunk man, crying and hovering near the gate.

"But I live in there!" he kept saying.

From his scruffy appearance, I thought, at first, he must be a homeless person who had been displaced from the Lower Manhattan area he usually wandered. But something about him didn't quite fit the profile of a derelict. Because he hadn't cleaned up in so long, he looked like a transient, and yet he had the pins from what looked like all the city's police precincts on his baseball cap, more than I'd ever seen. No transient would have been given those treasured pins or found such a cap in a trash bin. So I approached him, introducing myself. His name was Andrew, and in a few seconds, I heard his story. He was one of the equipment operators. He worked on a grappler, a piece of machinery that resembles a steel dinosaur with its long neck and serrated jaw that "bit" chunks off the pile. He told me of seeing things he couldn't shake, such as body parts in the jaws of his grappler and, worst of all, a baby's body.

He had been there since Day One, living at the site. That was my worst fear for these guys, that they really weren't leaving ground zero. Many of these construction workers, by choice, are transitory in their lifestyle. They go from job to job and sometimes even live out of their vehicles, saving as much money as they can. Andrew had managed to eat and sleep at the nearby Red Cross respite center without anyone noticing.

That day, however, almost two months after the attack, he finished his shift, drank a few beers, and basically fell apart. He was on the verge of a nervous breakdown, the first signs of which look similar to intoxication. When he'd tried to reenter ground zero, he had been dismissed from the job site and had his badge taken away until he "slept it off." But he kept hovering by the gate because he had nowhere to go. At risk of losing his job if he didn't "sleep it off," he couldn't go to the only sleeping quarters he'd known for two months. Andrew was just a man who had reached his limit. I talked to the police officers about what I feared was the truth about Andrew's demeanor, then I left them talking to him, hoping they would work it out. An hour later, I was happy to see him in the Red Cross respite center, walking into a room full of recliners, many of which held sleeping relief workers.

Without a support group, especially when every minute is money, workers at a disaster site are almost guaranteed not to know when enough is enough. But in disaster work, you have to protect yourself so you don't also become a casualty of the event. The enormous scale of the devastation—what needed to be moved and how long it would take to move it all—had made demolition work take center stage, however, so more construction workers were at the site now than ever before.

It's hard to describe the sheer volume of the pile. Move three beams, and three million more still need to be moved. Take three beams off the pile, put them in a dump truck, and the truck is full. Such a truck can carry tons, yet three beams were each truck's limit—their weight was that great.

The human body has a point when it can't carry any more weight as well. Sometimes the weight is emotional, sometimes it's physical, but like the trucks, there's a limit to what any body can carry.

Hitting overload can also happen to those of us in compassionate crisis work. It is why I've learned to take care of myself at any event, knowing the alternative. Occasionally, though, one of my team members learns his or her personal weight-bearing capacity the hard way. One of our volunteer chaplains, after five full days of giving his all on ground zero's night shift with little sleep, could not get out of bed. Something wasn't right, he said. He couldn't move. "I can't focus anymore in there, it's so ugly." He slept for an entire day, and then, as he began serving in other ways, he regained his perspective. Only experience can teach the warning signs, and few of us, thank God, have gone through enough traumas to recognize the signs for ourselves.

The normal ebbs and flows of morale were hard enough to handle. But as the next "wave" broke hard, morale plunged at the work site.

October 4, 2001
. . . Every day a new need or group is identified. Today the Red Cross began offering help for the thousands of families who must deal with death certificates to be entitled to benefits.

By the weekend, the recovery of bodies dried up again. All week, the rubble had been giving back bodies. The numbers of the identified were climbing daily in the published reports. And then, as quickly as it had started, it stopped. As the third week turned into a painful fourth, the fourth wave arrived: Emergency workers began to grasp that even the recovery of remains was going to be slim. We were not going to find the vast majority of the victims, dead *or* alive.

Rescue workers had been feverishly envisioning almost six thousand people to rescue. It would still be several more weeks before a more accurate tally would make the toll 2,823. Whatever the correct amount, it was still, as Mayor Rudy Guiliani first expressed it, "more than any of us can bear." For the ground zero worker, though, the significant count was recovered bodies to return to their families, and we had begun to suspect that tally would be inexpressibly low. It soon became obvious that we would not be able to identify more than a thousand of the victims of the World Trade Center attack through recovered remains. Less than a fourth of the missing would be positively identified. The heat of the explosion had created a mass cremation beyond comprehension. That meant no remains existed for thousands of victims; no positive IDs would be made to help those families accept their loved ones' deaths.

In the wake of a disaster comes a flood of paperwork. Families who suddenly have no way to pay bills need insurance payouts immediately. But that can't happen without death certificates. So in New York City, Red Cross bereavement centers began giving volunteer legal counsel to help victims' families cope with the needed affidavits, as well as offering thirty-thousand-dollar bereavement grants, no questions asked. The Red Cross prepared for thousands of responders. Yet only about a thousand people came. Most families were still not ready to acknowledge in such a final way, financial problems or no, that they had deaths to certify. As long as there was no body, there was hope—that must have been the unconscious mind-set of so many loved ones.

But since we now knew that no remains of any kind would be found for the majority of victims, Mayor Guiliani and his staff made a major move to help the citizens handle this mass loss. It was time for the victims' families to visit ground zero, to allow them to see why they would probably never have anything physical to identify and mourn.

A sophisticated Red Cross operation complete with chaplains and mental health experts was put into motion. Families of the missing could register for ferry rides from the bereavement center at Pier 94 on the west side of Manhattan to the harbor nearest the World Trade Center site. From there, they were taken by police escort inside the work site. A stand had been built overlooking ground zero so that they could safely visit and watch. The families were allowed to stay awhile, even have a prayer time if so desired. But most of all, they were now allowed to watch the work that would help them grasp the magnitude of what was going on and the grim reality of what had happened.

Every duty of this tragedy was a hard one, but what may have been the hardest duty of all, even beyond Fresh Kills or morgue duty, was being with the family members, seeing their faces as they stepped onto the platform and beheld the site for the first time. The sound of thousands of feet climbing the wooden platform's steps is one I'll never forget—*tap, tap, tap, tap.* Some stopped to write notes to their loved ones on the soft wood, openly sobbing. Others created their own memorials on the way with teddy bears, flowers, cards, and letters tacked here and there. The platform became an instant shrine covered with such remembrances. Some were saying good-bye, a final acceptance: *John, we love you and miss you. You will forever be in our hearts.* Others reflected family members still living in the comfort of denial, even there at ground zero: *Ellen, come home quickly, we need you. Please return to your family.* I understood this dynamic. Anything was better than facing the awaiting pain.

During the 1992 school shooting in Olivehurst, California, a hostage situation, we had been called in to work with the assembled parents as they waited to hear whether their sons and daughters would make it out alive. The tension had been excruciating as the hours ticked by, but for those parents, the cruel waiting had been better than the unwavering truth of a dead child. So must it have been for some New York family members holding their personal anguish at bay, especially without the finality of a loved one's body.

The teddy bears at the site were especially poignant. They had come as gifts from the people of Oklahoma City. The stuffed bears had been a symbol of the 1995 domestic terrorist bombing of the Murrah Federal Building; each of the victims' families had been given one. On the streets of Manhattan, a few days before the visits commenced, I had bumped into an old friend.

"Ray, good to see you." It was Jack Poe, an Oklahoma City Police Department chaplain, the senior chaplain at the Oklahoma City disaster site to which our team had reported.

"Here we are again," I said, but both of us agreed the situation at ground zero was worse than either of us had expected. "Where do they have you?"

"I'm on my way to pick up teddy bears sent from Oklahoma," he answered. "Five thousand of them. When the families go from the family bereavement center to ground zero, we want them all to have one to hold."

I was glad to hear it. As unusual as it may sound, teddy bears are quite an effective tool in compassionate crisis work. The stuffed bears give survivors and victims' family members something to hold on to as they do the grim, required things demanded of them—visiting the site, filling out forms, even identifying their loved ones. Sometimes it also gives them something to leave, an action that in itself is also a comfort.

I saw Jack's work all along the visitor platform, but especially at the harborside entrance to ground zero. During the next few days, a line of teddy bears began to form there, some with cards and notes, others with photos. For me, it was a daily reminder that the simplest things can offer the greatest meaning and comfort.

The atrocity's mass cremation was now undeniable. Yet even cremations offer something to help the families mourn: ashes. So, in a gesture that spoke poignantly of the communal nature of this massive event—so many dying in one place, so many individuals' ashes coming to rest on the same piece of ground—city officials planned another memorial service for the families. This time the families would be offered all that was left to offer, cremation containers full of ashes from ground zero itself. Perhaps this, city officials argued, would give families who would never have a body to bury something tangible to grieve over, something to acknowledge a death in order to go on with life.

The next Sunday afternoon, victims' families were again invited inside ground zero to receive an American flag and an urn of ashes. I recall most wrenchingly the reactions of one dead fire-fighter's young sons. One of the boys grasped the concept, saying it helped him a lot. But the other, younger, son had asked, "How do I know this is my dad?" Children have their own special issues, and they express them in unique ways. The effort, though, was a vivid acknowledgment of the need to help everyone begin the grief process, somehow, some way.

October 5, 2001
. . . Twenty-five thousand people escaped. This was the message that was delivered yesterday at ground zero. With so much death, the miracle of how many who'd escaped death had gotten lost. It was the largest successful rescue operation in American history.

Also that week, a report began to circulate around ground zero. The estimated number of people rescued in or near the buildings on September 11 was announced. The attack's devastating death toll had taken our focus so fully that we were not aware that the largest and most successful disaster rescue operation in the history of the United States also occurred that morning. At first, officials believed that almost twenty-five thousand people had escaped.

The announcement was meant to boost morale at a point when the fourth wave of the crisis was threatening to engulf both families and workers. Later reports would lower the actual survivor number. Almost everyone who could get out *did* get out, according to all reports. Due to the early timing of the plane crashes and the amount of vacant offices awaiting occupancy or remodeling, the survivor tally was closer to ten thousand, but the figure was still remarkable and the rescue operation still the largest in U.S. history. Credit was given to stairwells designed larger than codes required and to the towers' overall quality construction.

Because of a 1945 incident in which a B-52 bomber had hit the Empire State Building, the Twin Towers had been built to withstand the impact of a jetliner, albeit a 1973 jetliner, a generation removed from the 2001 commercial jets. But especially credited were changes made after the 1993 World Trade Center attack—emergency lighting installed, actual fire drills observed, and every handicapped employee given a wheelchair lightweight enough for two men to carry. The original announcement of the massive rescue effort helped families and workers alike cope with the fact that it was over, and so was most of the recovery.

But I knew from experience that we now faced the next phase—coping with grief. It would be, in actuality, the disaster's fifth wave. The way everyone coped with loss, from the child who lost his firefighter dad to the CEO whose company lost hundreds of workers, was the next struggle of this act of war. And this phase would be with us for a long time. A "wave" image is a fitting one; grief is a process that comes in waves. It wasn't going to end because we had memorial services or were urged to get back to normal by our national leaders. We knew this truth from the Oklahoma City disaster. Jack Poe had mentioned the situation when I'd seen him. The September 11 attack had opened up old wounds believed to have healed for many victims of the 1995 domestic terrorist attack. According to news reports, in the week after September 11, Oklahoma's mental health department hotline received triple its normal volume of calls.

On some levels, the whole country was affected. Even as a semblance of normalcy returned, even as we coped with the reality of a new war on terrorism, an underlying current of grief would manifest itself in our daily lives. If Oklahoma City's experience was any indication of the impact of this fifth wave, then we would be contending with collective grief as well as individual grief for years to come. If predictions based on a 1999 study of the Oklahoma survivors are accurate, almost half the people who were in Lower Manhattan on September 11 will have psychiatric problems, and a third of them will have posttraumatic stress disorder. Six years from now, many victims' families and survivors will still be in counseling. Rescue workers will only have begun asking for help.

Our modern culture has acquired an unhealthy view of grief, thinking it can be controlled, that it's a thing that we can and should get over quickly: We've got to get rid of the body, get past the funeral, get over it all, and get back to work. But if survivors and victims' families aren't given permission to grieve, they'll develop what we call "chronic grief." They'll be stuck in the first part of the process and never move forward. The result will be a group of people who will be alive physically but dead emotionally and spiritually. Chaplaincies as part of police and fire services have grown in the last fifteen years due to the recognition of this dynamic. A loved one's traumatic death can cause psychological damage that could play out devastatingly, sometimes months and years in the future. In Oklahoma City's bombing, 168 people died. Since then, six people, either survivors or victims' loved ones, have committed suicide. Statistically, the number of suicides-in-waiting from a disaster with thousands of victims is heart-stopping.

After September 11, some of the victims would find unique outlets for their grief that would help not only themselves but others, in the time-honored healing ways of community. Two stories reported in the national media during those first post attack days will forever stay with me. An Oklahoma City man who lost a daughter in the 1995 bombing volunteered to go to New York City to help. Sponsored by the Red Cross, he came, and three times a day, he escorted grieving family members on tours of ground zero. According to the *Time* magazine account, he felt it was important to show people that he was still standing, six years later. He had battled depression for three years before controlling it. Going to New York was his way to avoid "getting sucked back into the vortex of grief."

In Washington, D.C., a woman who lost a loved one in the attack on the Pentagon building reportedly walked into a nearby coffee shop and paid, in advance, the coffee and doughnut bill for the soldiers working the cleanup. She found a way to mourn uniquely and healthily by reaching out. The *Life* magazine account recorded the reaction of one air force officer: "I have no answers to how someone cultivates a heart as large as that."

These stories signaled to me that the event's grief, and its healing promise, had begun. And I knew that every resource we could muster should be focused on promoting such healthy grieving.

October 5, 2001
. . . . Counseling today at the college. A man told me he witnessed fifteen people jump or fall to their deaths. He didn't eat for several weeks, and he still does not sleep or rest comfortably. He asked, "What do I do with these images?"

The beginning of this fifth wave of the World Trade Center disaster seemed best exemplified by the cross-section of citizens we counseled at a college only a few yards from ground zero. For over a week, we had been splitting our time between working with faculty, staff, and students at the college and working C-watch with the ground zero relief workers. It began simply enough as a perceived need, as this work often does. The week before, while comparing notes with a chaplain we'd met at ground zero, he'd asked if we were CISM-trained. Critical Incident Stress Management training is one of the many training specialties essential for the compassionate crisis professional. Yes, I assured him. I had advanced CISM training in peer support and children's issues, and I had done thousands of debriefings—a better term for our service than the word "counseling."

"How can we help?" I asked.

The city college nearest the site, the Borough of Manhattan Community College (BMCC), had been closed since September 11 after one of its buildings was knocked down by the Twin Towers' collapse. "They believe six of their students may have been lost, but they don't fully know yet," he explained. "They're scheduled to open again tomorrow morning—seventeen thousand students and two thousand faculty members are returning. And their leaders have asked for chaplains to be there for counseling help."

So we decided to leave C-watch early that night in order to be on the BMCC campus for the first day of school. As expected, the faculty, staff, and students were heavily traumatized. The college officials set up rooms for us along with a schedule. For the next ten days, we would be available to talk to faculty, students, and staff members in whatever way they needed. Respecting the distance officially mandated for religion in a public school, as was appropriate, we were careful to help those who came to us in their personal contexts. Faculty and administrators came. They knew they were about to face classes full of young people who would want to talk about what had happened, and they asked for help with what to say and how to say it.

And their own trauma also needed to be expressed. One staff member captured the essence of what most people felt that day.

The horror of the number of deaths wasn't known at the moment of the attack. For those in Lower Manhattan that morning, witnessing the event was the first trauma. And the mercy of strangers would be the first wonder. The staff member had been on the street when the first plane hit. She froze, unable to turn her eyes from the fire above. When the second plane hit, she realized the city was under attack.

"I felt like a rat in a maze," she said. "I was convinced that there was nowhere I could run in the city. I couldn't go to Penn Station. I knew the next plane was going to hit there. I couldn't go to the Empire State Building—that was surely targeted, too. I couldn't go to the bridges because they could be blown up at any time. I couldn't go into the subways because the trains might stop, and we would be killed underground." She realized she had to go somewhere. But where? The Twin Towers were so tall they could crush five blocks in whatever direction they fell, and she was only two blocks away. Yet she could not move. "I live in Brooklyn, four hours on foot from here," she said. "All I could think to do was call my family on the phone and tell them I loved them. When I got off the phone, I just collapsed in the street. 'God!' I remember crying, 'why do I have to die today?'"

Then she felt someone grab her arm. "Quickly," a woman commanded her. "You're not going to die today. Come on!" She and this stranger began to rush away from the smoke and fire. "This woman walked me all the way home," the staff member explained. "For four hours, she stayed with me, and we didn't die. She left me at my house, and she went on to hers. And I made a promise to God as we walked: 'If you'll keep me alive just this day, I'll find out all I can about you.' So I just want to learn, Chaplain. I want to know about God."

Three students who came together also were memorable. Grief is as unique as the individual. Even when the loss or catastrophe experienced is the same, the responses can be vastly different. The three students, two sisters and a boyfriend, reminded me of that fact. The older sister was the reason they were there. She wanted to talk, her sister didn't, and the boyfriend wanted nothing to do with us. He was only along because his girlfriend had forced him to come.

The older sister began to talk, handing me a snapshot of a friend who'd earned an internship at a Twin Towers company and was now missing. When the first plane hit, the three of them had been outside the school. As they were standing there, staring at the fire above them, the second plane hit, and they watched as people fell to their deaths.

Thinking how horrific this must have been for such young eyes, I had to ask, "Did you see them hit?"

Mercifully enough, there was a building in front of their view. "We could see them falling, and then nothing." But she still felt guilty. "Why didn't I look away?" she asked.

Then the first tower collapsed, and they ran for their lives.

I glanced at the boyfriend sitting sullenly next to the two sisters. He looked as if he wanted to run from this conversation as fast as he had run from the dust cloud.

The older sister began to goad her younger sister into talking, but she refused. "Why do I want to talk about it?" she kept saying. Finally she admitted, all but stuttering, "I can't talk about it because I don't know how to! How can I possibly tell you . . . what words could I even . . . I just can't!"

What words can I tell you to describe what I'm feeling? That's what she was saying. Her response is one often experienced by children survivors. Adults assume that if children affected by a disaster are safe and quiet, they are fine. But the truth is they haven't developed a vocabulary to express their emotions. And these students were still children, no matter what they might have said to the contrary.

The students were three human beings trying to figure out their grief. They reacted in the ways most people do to personal loss—some don't want to talk about it, some do, and some say, in effect, "Let me get away; let me deal with it in my own way. Let me go punch a wall, so I don't hurt anyone."

The school nurse, however, may have said the most profound thing that any disaster survivor has ever said to me. We met at a special lunch arranged by a senior administration official just for us to have a chance to talk with her. Her expression of grief was a mixture of guilt, reflection, and responsibility. This nurse was the mom on campus. She was a fireball—a short, red-headed mother of a college-age kid herself who was always there for the students. She was willing and able to help them deal with the most intimate subjects, from problem pregnancies to abuse. She had been one of the last people to leave the campus on the morning of September 11, because she had to make sure everyone else got out. Yet that first day back on the campus, she was walking around in her white coat without a clue about what to say to the students she knew would be soon filling her office. I asked what the hardest part of the experience was for her.

"The hardest part is the guilt that I feel," she answered. "I have such an amazing amount of guilt."

That stopped me. "You mean, survivor's guilt?" I asked, knowing she would understand the term as a clinician.

"No, no," she had answered.

"You're not Muslim or Arabic, so it isn't national guilt, right?" I guessed. "What kind of guilt are we talking about?"

"I figure it this way, Chaplain. God didn't do this. Those men had a choice to do this and did it. But I feel equally responsible for this because I'm part of the human race," she said. "They actually believed they were doing it in the name of God, so convinced they were right they gave their lives for it. But how can I say I couldn't have been just as deceived as they were? I keep thinking of all the times that I chose my own way, too, and told God the way things should be."

For this nurse who dealt daily with other people's problems brought on by wrong choices, small and large, this was a crisis of bad decisions. And her own unique grief perspective was one that brought her to a place of deep personal reflection.

We are made to grieve our losses. In whatever form it takes, grieving is a normal, natural part of the healing process—the body's protection system, its way of coping. It must be given its due.

To talk about grief, though, is to talk about death. And usually, those who have trouble talking to others in crisis situations, worrying about what to say and how to say it, haven't dealt with their personal feelings about death. Yet death is the topic that never goes away during a disaster.

And, this side of a nihilistic, nothing-matters view of life that few people on 9/11 could bear to embrace, there aren't a lot of ways to talk about death without creating a spiritual dialogue. Wherever there is death, there is the question of God. My world-view is obviously Christian. That fact is displayed prominently by my collar and the cross on my helmet. For the people I encountered, however, the perspectives were as varied as those expressing them. Beyond the wealth of various religious beliefs, some might have a metaphysical perspective of death, others a purely psychological view. But since my perspective on death was biblical, it was all I could offer. Although respectful of other perspectives, I always explain that fact to anyone broaching the subject with me in a crisis setting. While some may try to draw me into a theological discussion, it is really not why I am there and usually not what people truly desire. They want answers that somehow bring comfort. So spiritual conversations in a disaster's aftermath are really about whether a person's religious convictions meet the intense needs of the moment. In short, does one's faith work?

If I further an ongoing dialogue that an individual is having with his or her own belief system, then my part in that person's spiritual crisis is a good one. Any other reasons for such a discussion in that context are about ego, not service. But that doesn't mean such moments don't offer surprises.

The best example of this began as a loud encounter outside the Union Square subway station. As I was about to enter the station, a young woman suddenly yelled in my direction, "I hate you and what you stand for! I hate all religions! They're the reason that all these people died!"

She was a young African-American woman. Behind her stood an older woman, quiet, nervous, and embarrassed. The pair were obviously mother and daughter. The mother was a Christian, I learned, but she could only stand by as her daughter vented her frustrations on the collar around my neck and the cross on my uniform for all the ills of religious fanaticism. I guessed that I had just become a part of an old issue between the pair. For all I knew, I was the latest in a long line of chaplains, pastors, and priests she had confronted since September 11.

But I only had a short time with her, I knew. My task was not to strike up a street debate, but to attempt to give her a new slant on an old theme. I was there to offer the same service as I did for the woman on the ferry who was locked in a memory. I could nudge her stalled thinking with a different angle of thought—something that might give comfort in a new way, which might help her move past her anger. Because no argument, even one she won, was going to salve her wounds that day.

So I chose to look at her need, and what I saw seemed to include her mother. "I understand exactly how you feel," I said. "The answers we all need may be impossible to know right now, but I tell you one thing. You love your mom, right?"

She glanced at her mother. "Yes."

"How long would be enough to be able to be with her? Fifty years?"

"Yes, that'd be great."

"How about if it could be forever?"

She paused. "You're talking about heaven, aren't you?"

"It's one of the good things about your mom's faith: life after death—no matter how death comes or when," I answered. "If you're right about all religions, there's nothing ahead to hold on to. But if your mother's faith in Christ is right, then you'll always be with her. There's not a whole lot more to the choice, really."

The young woman, surprised at the direction the conversation had taken, said nothing.

A rose vendor approached us. Normally I would never have bought one, but that day, I did. "Here, this is for you." I held it out to the young woman.

She took it, her eyes softening, reddening a bit. "I'll place it on the memorial." She took a step toward one of the makeshift memorials at the subway station entrance.

"No, no," I said. "That's for you. Press it in a book, and years from now you'll find it, and you and your mom will remember this night."

I left mother and daughter talking as I descended into the subway station. Most of my chats were like that, some shorter, some longer. Whatever number of knocks is needed to open a door still results in an open door, even if I'm not the one who knocked last. This time, however, I was offered a peek inside one of those doors. About twenty minutes after I'd left the two and gone into the subway system, I was still there, reading a memorial wall. Sometimes during those weeks, it could take me an hour to walk a block since I was talking to so many people and stopping at so many homemade memorials. As I was reading the tribute to a port authority officer erected as a shrine outside his duty station, I felt a tap on my shoulder. It was the daughter. And she was suddenly giving me a big hug. "I just wanted to catch you, to tell you that, well, I still have lots of questions, but the answers don't seem as hard. Thank you."

As she rushed away, I don't mind telling you that I was suddenly the one with red eyes.

Most questions about God, in the aftermath of tragedy, are really about dealing with death, I've learned. The reality of a deadly catastrophe seems to imply that God hid his face, ran away, left the scene—the presumption being that the absence of God allowed the tragedy to happen: If God be God, where was God? If God was here, then how could this happen? This was the biggest spiritual obstacle people expressed after September 11. It is the age-old question asked in the aftermath of every atrocity of history: Where was God? The twentieth century's Jewish Holocaust, whose number of casualties and depth of evil continues to boggle the mind, is perhaps the best example. To feel a sense of God in joyous moments of life seems natural. But we cannot imagine why or how a loving God could be present during suffering of any kind.

Yet how can we explain the stories told of God's presence amid such horrors as the Holocaust? And how do we explain the stories that survivors of September 11 have told—of small choices or still, small voices keeping them home, making them late to work, or leading to a stairwell in the dark? Emergency service personnel talk of the things they have heard over their radios. In an emergency, radio channels remain open, allowing officials to talk without pushing buttons. It also allows them to hear the drama happening behind the open radio transmitters. Many talk about having heard both hysteria and calm—the evoking of God's help and the grasping of God's peace. Such true stories put God right in the midst of tragedy, in the midst of death as well as life.

Beth, the detective I met at sunrise one morning, had lived while rescue workers beside her had died. Life and death were a matter of inches. She had come back every morning to that same spot trying to understand why she was spared. Survivor's guilt was consuming her. For some people in this situation, the only conversation that gives comfort is one that helps them be consistent with their thinking. Beth was one of those.

"Why did God do this?" she'd asked.

I explained what I believed—that such evil was against the nature of a creator I called my "heavenly Father."

"Then why did God allow it?" If God could have stopped it and didn't, this survivor had to believe that something was wrong with us or something was wrong with God.

Beth and I, sitting there in the morning sun, explored the very basics of the Christian faith and its mystery—our free will, God's sovereignty, God's grace. Yet despite all the theological talk, she still could not get past the deaths that had occurred so near her. It was the memory that had her locked tight. "But those people standing right by me," she said. "What about them?"

Throughout all I've seen in this work, all the things I've heard, and all the things I trust, there is one belief I rest in. It is what allows me to keep doing this work, no matter how grim it becomes. And that belief, I realized, was what would give Beth the comfort she needed.

I told her where I believed God was during the disaster.

"Let's say you're right and that God did allow this to happen," I began. "To have such influence, that would mean God is all-powerful, right?"

"Yes . . . ," she agreed.

"Then, in the time the buildings were hit and then collapsed, can you believe that God was also powerful enough to help every single one of the people who died?"

At that, she paused. She was silent for a long moment, then tears came to her eyes. "You mean if God could have helped them to live, then he could have helped them to die?"

"God could have wrapped his arms around every single one," I said, "and helped them go into eternity. Even those who may have lived on the pile for several days before dying, he could have been right there in the ruins with them."

She gazed back at the spot where the ones around her had died, and so did I.

The struggle still existed, I admitted to her. We still had a choice—to believe that a God big enough to allow a disaster was also big enough to help everyone affected, or to believe that either

God wasn't big enough or that He didn't care. "Believing one will bring you peace; the other one will bring you hopelessness," I added. "But anybody who would come back here for fourteen days straight already knows the answer."

It didn't matter whether Ray Giunta or anybody else came to New York after September 11 announcing that God was there, offering piously pat answers for the spiritual hunger that was everywhere. What really mattered was the testimony of those who felt God's presence and lived to tell about it, be it a still, small voice showing them the way out of a subway or the mercy of fellow survivors who walked them all the way home.

But what matters most of all is the hope of God's presence for those who did not live to tell about it.

We will never fully know what happened in the thousands of different lives that ended that day. Firefighters often talked about those who survived the collapse but could not be reached in time, the rubble too massive to be moved before they died. But I have to believe that in those awful moments, whether it was an hour, three days, or ten, those people did not die alone, that God in His love and His compassion was right there with them. And when they breathed their final breaths—in that hallowed moment, He was *most* present of all.

The struggle we humans have with the issue of death comes from being unable to see death as God must see it. A God-perspective of death is not one we humans easily embrace—that death is a part of life, even when it is at the hands of other human beings. I recall reading a statistic during that time, stating that seven thousand Americans die each day. Death is something we all will face, but to God death isn't a terrible thing. In the Christian tradition, it's actually a graduation. According to my faith system, it is a continuance of life because of faith in Christ, a moving into God's presence with all the joy that promises. Or, as I've expressed the thought at many memorial services, death is not a period, but a comma.

If there's a message from God through this disaster, it has to be that this life isn't everything. There's a whole life beyond this life, a whole existence beyond this planet. This isn't our home. Why else do people go with reckless abandon into burning buildings and unstable girder pockets? Because they have a healthy understanding that death is not always to be feared above all, above everything.

There is something beyond death that makes such acts possible. The "peace that passes understanding" that we all pray to have in the middle of sorrow starts with having that proper perspective about death. If you have that, you can go into those buildings, and you can stand on a moving pile of twisted beams. You can help in ways you could never help without that peace. I realize I could die serving people in just this way, doing exactly what New York Fire Department Chaplain Father Mychal Judge was doing when he died in the first minutes of the attack. I can say that I even expect it. So I don't worry about it, because that healthy understanding of death is one I feel deep in my bones.

Probably one of the most powerful moments that I experienced at ground zero was one rainy, messy night in October during a shift spent combing through pieces in a stairwell. It was the sixth or seventh rain since the attack. Along with a team of firefighters and ESU members, I was on my hands and knees digging with my short-handled shovel for remains. During a pause, in which we had to stand back while a heavy machine cut away a section of the pile, a big, burly African-American police officer put a hand on something in his pants pocket. He fingered it a moment, then pulled it out. It was one of the little Gideon Bibles. And when he spoke to me, it was through a jaw set as hard as stone.

"Father," he began, assuming from my collar, like so many others, that I was a Catholic priest, "I know the Good Book says I'm supposed to forgive, to turn the other cheek, but I'm sorry, I just can't do that. I'm too angry. I don't know what to do I'm so mad."

"Well, I'm standing here, and I'm mad, too," I said. "Just stop for a minute and look around. Look at this mess! You're mad, I'm mad, God's mad!"

He squinted hard at me. "Are you saying that *God* is angry?"

"You bet. How could the Creator of the universe not disapprove of this? You better believe there's a place for righteous anger." I waved at the enormity of where we were standing, at the evilness of it all. "What do you think God is thinking right now? Here, God gave us freedom to make our own choices, and we use it to fly planes into buildings and kill innocent people. If you ask me, I think God is very angry we would use our freedom to do something so horrible." I stopped to wipe the rain off my face. "You want to know something? You've shed a few tears over all this, right?"

"Right."

"Me, too. Well, all this rain since the attack, it just keeps feeling to me like God's tears crying over this place. I can't get that image out of my head. I'm crying, you're crying, God's crying. You know?"

"So are you saying that God is okay with me being angry?" he said, still finding it hard to believe.

"Listen," I answered, "the fact that you're asking about being close to God is enough, but your being here, angry or not, that says it all. You just have to know how to handle it. Are you sleeping when you're off-duty?"

"No, I'm not really sleeping. All I do is think about this."

"It's really important that you know how to handle your stress," I told him. "Your family needs you to be well, and so do your 'brothers' out here. You need to take care of yourself, drink plenty of water, and remember to eat. That will help you deal with the way you feel. It helps me."

Neither of us spoke for a moment. And in the lull, as heavy machinery rolled by us, the pile moved under our feet. It did that a lot during those days. Everyone there came to feel the pile was very much alive with its steam and its heat and its rumbling and groaning. But this movement was like a minor earthquake. It rumbled and shook hard. Most of the time you made sure you were ready for it, but we had been talking so intently that we were both caught by surprise. I looked at him, and he looked at me.

"Wow," I gasped as both of us got our balance again. Then, joking, I added, "Hey, if it falls in, just grab onto my arm, because I'm ready."

He looked puzzled. "What?"

"I mean, I know where I'm going if this thing falls in and takes us with it. I'm going to heaven. I'm ready."

Then he started to laugh. It was one of those hard laughs, a mixture of anger and irony and surprise. He laughed so hard I started to wonder.

"Man, that's amazing!" he finally said. "The message in my life just never seems to change. I played football in high school, in college, and I even played some semi-pro ball. And the one thing every coach I had told me was to be ready. They drilled it—I had to get ready. When I grew up, I got married; I wasn't ready to be a husband. So I had to get ready. When I had a son, I wasn't ready to be a father, so I had to get ready. Now I'm standing here in this place with all this death, and you tell me, I've got to get ready to die?" He shook his head as he steadied his balance on the pile. "Not until right now did I think I needed to get ready to meet my Maker."

"I'm sure you're more ready than you think," I said.

"No, I'm not ready, Father," he said. "I mean, I'm a religious man, I guess, but I don't know about being ready to die."

"Well," I said, "you can get ready. It's real simple. God's taken care of it."

"What do you mean?"

I pointed to the pocket Bible he was still holding inside his big fist. "Being ready isn't being religious. The way your Good Book right there explains it, you're ready if you just believe in the Lord and tell people what you believe. Remember the story about the thief on the cross next to Christ?"

"Yeah. Where is it?"

I turned to the story and showed him. "The thief didn't have time to get ready. He was dying, just like Christ. All he did was acknowledge his need and say he believed who Christ was. And Christ responded by saying that the man would be in paradise with Him that day. So—do you believe?"

"Yeah, I do."

"Okay. You're ready."

The cop stood there a second, staring at me. I could almost see his thoughts churning. Then he pocketed the little Bible, turned, and stepped back to the area he'd been working before we started talking, as if he didn't need me anymore. And perhaps he didn't. Those few minutes were the essential reason for a chaplain to be there, the ministry of presence in its purest form, to leave the hope of God's love with the selfless workers in this horrible place, right when they needed it the most. I caught his eye—he gave me a thumbs-up. And we both went back to the work. Our talk had been one of those special, raw, holy moments offered by a living God big enough to be present in a place reeking of death. It would be a story to inspire and comfort both of us as we faced the grim job of uncovering victims' remains, and a story to cherish in the years ahead.

As I picked up my shovel, I looked at the pile below us, and my heart ached for the victims. I thought about life and death, about anger and peace, about courage and presence. At the very depths of my faith is the need to believe that God was big enough to be there for those who must have waited for death on the floors above and the collapsed ruins below.

And I have to believe that in those stories we will never hear is the truth we cling to—that these innocent people were not only comforted but inspired by a God who was near.

October 5, 2001

. . . Today I met a man whose nephew was killed in the attack. Our heroes of this disaster have been those who ran in when others were running out, but after hearing this story I think perhaps we should expand the term.

The nephew worked for Cantor Fitzgerald, a company in the WTC that lost almost seven hundred employees. On September 11 he arrived early and took his place on the 105th floor. We don't know the details, but we know he was there when the plane hit the first tower. How do we know? Because his mother also worked in the building. On September 11 she was late and did not commute with her son as she usually did. As she was coming to the building, she received a page. The digital pager displayed an instant message sent from her son trapped high in the sky: "Do not come in or near the towers, Mom. I love you."

Many have wondered what those who were trapped did after the attack and before they lost their lives. For this heroic young man, we know: His thoughts were on his mother's safety.

Chapter Ten

Light Chasing Darkness

October 6, 2001–December 11, 2001

. . . As I am at ground zero this evening, a thought comes into my mind: How do those who lost a loved one in this place feel when they hear people say, "It's time to get back to normal"? What does it mean to return to normal? It is eerie to see right at the site of the disaster how people have moved on . . .

IN THE WEEKS BETWEEN SEPTEMBER 11 and December 11, 2001, I flew back and forth between California and New York City six times, sometimes with additional team members, sometimes alone. After my first three weeks there, I made much shorter visits to the disaster site, going home for a few days to refuel with my family and to "debrief" with the help of my partner, Jeff, before returning. Traveling all those overnight "red-eye" transcontinental flights, I was struck with how we were chasing darkness for hours and hours until finally catching up to the light. For the rest of my life, I doubt that I will be able to look out a plane's window without recalling the feeling of light chasing the darkness away, going to and from all those nights spent at ground zero.

The memories would invade my dreams—those nights, that darkness—like it would for almost everyone who had been there. I slept very little during those weeks in New York, only three or four hours a night, so I never really left the World Trade Center site even when I wasn't physically there. That would be true even when I returned home to California. For the first few nights lying in my own bed, I'd be back at ground zero in my dreams, walking the disaster area. But I was never dreaming of horrifying images. I was seeing people's faces, their flickers of light dispelling the darkness. And as I dreamed I'd be patting my wife on the back, saying, "God bless you for your work today . . . America loves you and supports you . . . Keep up the good work . . . God bless you."

After I would awaken her half a dozen times in one night, my long-suffering wife, Cathy, would pull me to her and whisper, "Ray, you're safe. You're home now."

EACH TIME I RETURNED TO MANHATTAN, the scene was different—and the same. I never failed to be touched by the *New York Times*'s ongoing biographical series of the disaster's victims called "Portraits of Grief." Its parade of photos and stories on each individual was always the same and always different. It continued for months and months, honoring each life for its special place now lost to the world. The names alone spoke of America's "melting pot" strength—from Gonzalez to Farrelly, from Peluso to

Chan, they were like a daily meeting with the face of democracy, as well as a reminder of why we continued to work.

I boarded a subway train at the height of rush hour on my first trip back. It was packed. Sardines aren't as crushed as we were. I had never seen a train so full. I am always amazed at how many people can squeeze into a New York subway car at rush hour; if the doors can close, then the car is good to go. That was the scenario. No one was happy; we were all cheek to jowl. To my far left, a woman had had all she could take.

"Stop pushing!" she said to the man behind her.

"I'm not pushing," he grunted.

"Stop *pushing!*" she repeated, louder.

"I'm not the one doing it! I'm not pushing!" he said.

"You *are* doing it! Stop pushing!" she said, now yelling. "STOP PUSHING!"

"LADY—" the man yelled back, "WHY DON'T YOU GO STRAIGHT TO *HEAVEN!*"

For an instant, everyone in the car went silent. Then all of us burst out laughing. We knew full well how such a statement was usually phrased. But not that day in New York City. Even the woman, as angry as she was, couldn't hold on to it after that.

In my entire life, I had never heard anything quite like that statement. I thought about what it meant. The disaster gave a whole city, famous for its brusqueness, the permission to be kind to one another. It would be the same for the entire nation. I firmly believe that the average person wants to do the right thing. Very few people would not consider helping someone in true need. It's just that everyday survival often buries that natural compassion. Yet when survival instincts should have ruled the day in New York City, the very opposite happened. How long would it last? It didn't matter. True hearts had been revealed.

On one of my trips, I brought back a special package that mirrored America's continued true-heart compassion as well. As many schoolchildren did in those weeks after the attack, my daughter Katie and her second-grade classmates drew precious pictures and wrote heartfelt words on cards to the ground zero workers. But, unlike other children, she and her schoolmates knew theirs would be going by special delivery, taken there in person. The most valuable cargo in my pack that trip were those homemade cards.

WITH EACH TRIP BACK TO NEW YORK, I went back to my old routine of keeping C-watch during the night, even though my days were filled with new crisis care work. Almost daily, I noticed changes at ground zero—changes in its complexity as well as its issues. Firefighters and police officers actually clashed the first week of November over the city's attempts to scale back the firefighters' slow, hands-on presence in favor of more heavy equipment work, until a compromise was found. The machine operators, caught in the middle, made a point of saying in news reports that they would not turn their backs on the firefighters even though their orders were now to continue work unless specifically ordered to stop. As a *Washington Post* article of the time explained, "in an unspoken pact," the excavators would dig, and if anything looked out of place, they would take the load and place it to the side for a firefighter search, as they went on to work on another area. It was good to see that camaraderie was still strong. I did begin to worry about what the workers had now begun to call the "cough" that came from their prolonged exposure to the concrete dust, diesel fumes, smoke, asbestos, and ground glass in the air.

By my last trip in December, the area outside the West Highway checkpoint had been transformed into a Manhattan winter wonderland including a Star of David, Christmas lights, a Christmas tree, a scaled replica of the World Trade Center Twin Towers, and other tributes to the ingenuity and devotion of the people of New York. When I had first seen this area, it was all but covered with debris from the collapse. New York was reclaiming itself gradually and determinedly. Only a few yards away, though, the work continued. Ground zero, by then, had become a reclamation and demolition site; the number of heavy equipment pieces on the scene had more than tripled. In early December, one of the stairwell entrances was uncovered along with a large group of victims, so close to escape, yet so far. Recovery, however slow, was still going on, despite the demolition site atmosphere. The work at ground zero did not even stop on Christmas Day as many workers volunteered to continue the search for one more body to give back to his or her family. One of the last nights I worked C-watch, we found another fireman, entombed by a large I-beam.

November 30, 2001

. . . Today I visited four firehouses. I noticed the "day shoes" worn between calls; on September 11, thirty-three men out of the four houses had left sixty-six shoes behind.

So much pain.

All gave some, some gave all.

During my first weeks at ground zero, I had met the chaplain and founder of Motor Racing Outreach, which works with racing professionals, including those of the popular NASCAR circuit. During one of my later trips, the chaplain had asked me to escort one of NASCAR's famous drivers, Dale Jarrett, around the ground zero area to encourage the firefighters and police officers. So I did, also taking him to visit a few of the firehouses. While we were visiting Engine 28, a call came in. We watched them rush to the fire truck, shed the "day shoes" all fire personnel wear between calls, don their "bunker" gear, including boots, then jump onto the fire engine and roll out, sirens blaring. As they disappeared from sight, I looked back at the shoes now forming an outline of the fire engine parked there only seconds ago. Suddenly I was imagining the same scene as it must have happened in firehouses across the city when the Twin Towers call came in.

Minutes later the fire engine, loaded with firefighters, was back. It had been a false alarm. As we watched, they got out of their boots and back into their day shoes.

But I couldn't shake the image of the hundreds of shoes that weren't reclaimed on September 11. I saw them lying on firehouse floors across New York City, until someone, a comrade or a friend, had to pick them up and put them forever away. And I was reminded of the shoes I had seen at the Holocaust Museum in Washington, D.C. History does repeat itself, in small ways as well as large.

December 2, 2001
. . . Today I met a local minister who said he had a burden for the bereaved and would like our help in launching a national ministry. When I asked him repeatedly how that would help the widows and orphans of NYC, he couldn't answer.

I am concerned for church pastors as the anticipation of a great American awakening created by September 11 events fails to materialize.

My work during the rest of the year was also different—and the same. Compassionate crisis work has two distinct phases that usually overlap. First, being fully involved in a disaster's relief work is the important task. Then, gradually, as the primary need abates, the focus shifts to analysis. We analyze what's been learned so we can apply the knowledge to the needs that will linger.

Preparing to handle grief issues, the disaster's "fifth wave," was now of prime importance. So many people and groups wanted to learn how to offer compassionate crisis care to their communities, we moved naturally and quickly into the second phase. Ten million people live in New York City alone, all of whom were survivors, in a very real sense, of the disaster. The lasting resources required were potentially more than the Red Cross and Salvation Army could handle, even more than governmental mental health agencies could handle. Only one group seemed large enough, because of its enormous volunteer capacity, to truly contain grief's tidal wave for the duration—and that was the church, synagogue, or temple on the corner.

"Pastoring the Pastors" was the title of a *New York Times* article on the myriad ways that Jewish and Christian leaders were attempting to guide their pastors and rabbis through what it called the "bewildering emotional and spiritual and liturgical questions" of the attack. Few had the training to deal with this level of crisis response, and, as one Episcopal bishop was quoted as saying, "Anyone who is a lone ranger is in dangerous shape." In response to this need, several We Care team members, including myself, began to teach, train, and speak. In fact, we had begun to do so by the second trip back. An early invitation to talk to 250 leaders representing a group of area churches was a good example. We had trained all sorts of organizations from corporations to churches over the years, but now we especially focused on responding to the many churches and church leaders who were asking for training.

During this time, I was asked to bring to ground zero other professionals who, for various reasons, needed the right perspective on the event. Yet I vowed it would be in a practical way, especially after seeing so many people visit the site only long enough to get a sound bite for their own use. So those who came with me became volunteer chaplains. They did not come just to look; they came to be of service, and they were. I especially recall a particularly blessed moment during one of those nights, and so would one of the volunteer chaplains with me named Bart. This certain visitor hadn't planned to be a volunteer, much less a chaplain. But he became one in the best way possible—he was willing to go. He was a perfect example of how anyone can practice the first essential step of the ministry of presence.

A California businessman and a devoted Christian, he had traveled to New York with several men who were meeting with me to talk about the ground zero work, never imagining he'd find himself inside the zone. When I invited the men to go with me to ground zero and be chaplains for the night, he was surprised but said he would help in any way God could use him. And that is what happened. I handed each one of the men a hard hat that prominently displayed the symbol of the chaplain's cross. After we arrived on the hill inside ground zero, I suggested the men go and talk with the firemen and policemen working that night on the pile. At first Bart had been overwhelmed with the idea, feeling inadequate to help the workers.

"What do I do?" he asked me.

"Just go up there and be with those men. You'll know what to do," I told him, confident that God would guide his actions and his words.

Later, Bart told me what happened as he did as I suggested.

Several members of the FDNY's Eighty-second Battalion approached him and laid four body bags at his feet. Then they all dropped to one knee and removed their helmets. That's when he realized they were waiting for him to pray. "I will never forget the honor of being in the presence of those men and praying for them and the remains of the souls within those bags," he told me. He would also remember every word of his prayer that night, and he shared those words with me. He had prayed, "What we stand on was one of the greatest buildings of all mankind, and because of the evilness of men it went down in tragedy. In those ruins we stand with these men, these rescuers, and out of that rescue will come redemption and restoration."

December 4, 2001

. . . Nothing religious about a patrol officer named Joe, just a genuine love for people and God. He had just prayed a silent prayer for some encouragement. When not one but four chaplains had appeared, he laughed. Funny thing, though, Joe encouraged me. God's still choosing to work through "flesh suits."

As I've said, God chooses to work through "flesh suits," through flawed, fragile human beings, for reasons the Creator of the universe only knows—people like police officers named Joe, like members of churches, temples, and synagogues, like volunteers at the Red Cross and Salvation Army, like a chaplain from California. He continues to use us, despite our mistakes.

And we continue to want to be used. We keep being drawn to places beyond our own backyards, beyond our own insecurities and our fears, beyond sights that can raise our own questions about our faith, and about God and humanity. And once there, we find that new meanings for old words draw most of us back again:

"Love your neighbor . . ."

"Love conquers fear . . ."

"The Lord is my shepherd . . ."

During my sixty-eight days working at ground zero, I worked with volunteer chaplains from Louisiana, Connecticut, Indiana, California, Canada, North Carolina, and Tennessee. I also talked to hundreds of people I would never see again, only a passing witness to so many unforgettable moments touched by God's grace. That is the best and the worst of this special work. For "flesh suits" who naturally crave knowing any story's end, such brief encounters are often difficult. But they keep our motives pure.

We are there just to love those in our path for the life in them, caring compassionately in the moment—because moments are all we really have.

DURING OCTOBER, ALONG WITH TWO of my volunteer chaplains, I was asked to address a group of leaders and speakers preparing for a convention the following day. It was going to be a gathering of a thousand counseling professionals, those who would soon be the ones coping with the emotional fallout of the coming wave of grief. Many of them were also connected to religious organizations.

We spoke last. By the time I began to speak, I found myself overwhelmed with all the raw emotion of the hundreds of people I'd met, the hundreds of pleas and questions I'd heard. I kept seeing the look in the firefighters' eyes as they held on tight to their pocket Bibles and their rage. And I knew that the usual responses, detached and formulaic, were not up to the challenge of the crisis I was seeing every day here. And when I finally spoke, I realized my own responses were not up to that moment, either. I couldn't bring myself to give my planned, expected, chaplain's report of work at ground zero. I found myself, instead, speaking short and to the point:

"I'm not going to tell you any stories," I said. "But I do want to tell you something that is going to make all the difference in the work you have ahead of you. First, this is a spiritual crisis, and, second, pat answers are not working. Not to be engaged in this experience, not to be in it with them in order to find answers that match the pain, is just wrong. It's insulting to God, insulting to the people of New York, and insulting to the world. Pray hard tonight for the words you will be saying to the convention's crowds. And if tomorrow you don't know what those words are, then I'll be at ground zero, and you can come into the pile with me and find them there."

To my utter surprise, one by one, almost half of the group approached me, wanting to volunteer, to see what I'd seen and feel what I felt. As I stood in the debris pile with these convention speakers and leaders who had taken my challenge, I recall thinking that some things cannot be put into words, that some empathy has to be earned. And I only wished I could take all the counseling professionals attending the convention into the searing experience for the benefit of the people soon to be asking for their help.

Later, I would be invited to put my thoughts into writing for the professional counseling association's publication. I began thinking of all the victims of the tragedy who were nowhere near the towers that morning, such as Pat, one of the tragedy's first suicides, the breast-cancer survivor who shot herself a month after her husband was killed at the World Trade Center. These were the hidden victims, the survivors, who needed their voices to be heard. And their voices were also the voices of victims everywhere, in the crises of everyday life around us. So I wanted to write a different sort of diary entry intended to help the helpers, a deeper reflection filled with the words left unsaid that night. But, as diaries often do, the writing of it also helped the writer:

. . . "Never Forget" says a banner at ground zero. We are torn between wanting to forget the worst thing that has ever happened to innocent people in America yet wanting to pay tribute to the memories of the individuals who died. How will we mark the anniversary date in the days, months, and years to come? We have seen nations come together in unprecedented ways. More than a billion dollars has been raised. Almost a million pints of blood were donated. Thousands of volunteers came, wrote, and prayed for the effort.

The new American anthem: *What can I do?*

I believe it is time to try something new ...

Most of us will never go to ground zero and serve the recovery workers. This is perfectly acceptable for two reasons: First, tremendous support systems are already in place for rescue professionals working there. Second, there are tens of thousands of others away from ground zero who desperately need our help.

We have already seen the first suicide following this disaster. It is too late to help those like Pat, but the message from her grave is a cry for help, an urgent appeal for us to refocus our energies from the barbaric events of September 11 to the thousands left behind who must find a way to move forward. And the same is true for victims of all of life's crises. We must ask the Pats of the world some important questions, and we must listen to their answers:

Who are you?

We come from every walk of life, every culture, and every socioeconomic status. We live in every city throughout America. We work, shop, and worship next to you each day. We sit next to you on planes, trains, and buses. Our children attend your children's schools, and we attend soccer games and movie theaters, just like you. Yet we are different. We carry around a silent pain . . .

What do you need?

The greatest thing we need is for you to educate yourselves about what we are feeling physically, emotionally, cognitively. Spiritually, we are at different places. But one thing is for sure: We don't expect you to have all the answers. We are caught in the pounding surf. Each attempt to escape brings another wave crash-

ing over us . . . It is not what you yell from the warm beach fire
that comforts us but the way you make your way through the
surging tide to meet us in the water. What we need most from you
is a listening ear. Listening, staying with us, not demanding the
impossible, gives us hope to endure.

What can we do?

Recognize that when you ask "What can I do?" you have
already done something. You have reminded us that we are not
alone and that people still do care.

. . . As we continue to ask and listen, we mark the anniversary
every day. In this we will be doing something different.

We will be remembering the living.

No one involved with the World Trade Center tragedy came
away untouched, and I was no exception. In the months following my autumn spent at ground zero, as I returned to my home
routine, I began to realize the personal impact of those New York
days and nights spent serving in this historic disaster event. Seeing
God in action in dozens of consecrated moments forever
changed me. I went to ground zero as a crisis chaplain; I came
home a changed Christian. I went as a professional minister,
counselor, and helper; I came home with an even more deeply
devoted heart for my spiritual life. I went to New York City with
a certain understanding about my place as a man of God. I came
home realizing I had much more to learn. I admitted to myself
that I had begun going through the motions in my personal life
and my crisis work. But after being part of what one friend called

"a story in motion about the gospel," I saw everything with new eyes. It was as if the headlines attached to all the turning points in my life also announced my spiritual growth spurts. Since those weeks at ground zero, I've made new commitments to my friends, my wife, my family, and my faith. I have had a renewed compassion and a bigger heart to know God's heart. I have had a deeper desire to pray, to know more about God's character. I have begun to wonder more consciously about God's thoughts, especially as they pertain to my actions. And I have remembered that we never are finished growing unless we stop looking for signs of God in all that we experience.

ON MY LAST SUNDAY IN New York City, I decided to attend church. In the middle of the service, as I was reflecting on these powerful days spent there and the humbling privilege of it all, I suddenly thought of a recurring dream of mine.

For years, I had been dreaming that I could fly. I would be walking, and all of a sudden, I'd lift off the ground. Sometimes I would fly around for short periods; other times, I wouldn't be able to get off the ground at all.

Then, as I continued to dream this dream, I began to fly more. And as I flew, I could see people, but they couldn't see me. And I never said a word to them.

That went on for months and months.

Then the dream progressed again. I began to fly farther and higher than ever before. To take off from the ground, I would simply feel light, and off I'd float. I would rise to amazing heights, yet I had no fear. I had total confidence in my ability to go wherever I wanted to go. And I could now not only see people but I could hear people going about their lives, even though they could still not see me.

After that, I didn't have the dream for a long time.

And when I dreamed it again, everything was different.

I was flying along large concrete walls forming a stone canyon. When I looked down to see what was below me, I noticed cars on what appeared to be a large freeway—eight lanes in one direction, all facing toward me. As I dropped down lower, I realized they were standing still. I flew for miles but still saw no movement below me. I dropped lower to gaze directly into the cars and saw the reason. The people in the cars were all dead. I saw no trauma, no gore of any kind; yet the people were silently still in the way that comes only in death.

My attention, then, was drawn upward, to the top of the concrete walls. I flew up to investigate. And there, as far as I could see, were people milling around the edges of the concrete canyon, masses of them, looking down at the cars. They were drinking, smoking, talking, eating, and acting as if everything were normal. And then they saw me. The crowd immediately began to call out to me as if I were some kind of hero or superhuman.

I was the God-man who could fly.

199

No, no, I quickly called out. *I have just been allowed to fly so you'd listen to what I'm supposed to say.* And then I began to tell them about the goodness and love of God.

I have never had that dream, or any dream about flying, again. Now I think I know why.

December 10, 2001
. . . The ruins of the last buildings are almost cleared. From the viewing platform, I glimpse a cross created by the demolition left standing by the workers until the very last moment. Because of God's grace and privilege, I've been allowed to serve another day.

InMemoriam

Ninety Days After

December 11, 2001

. . . Today was the ninetieth day since the World Trade Center attack.

Arriving at the security checkpoint on Broadway and Fulton, the scene had become familiar. People lining the streets with cameras, stretching and straining to get a peek at some part of what we call ground zero. Behind the police barricades stand a squad of New York's finest, the NYPD. I remember when the check would take a few minutes, but not on this day. Recognizing our faces, the officers waved us through and greeted us like family members

The drizzle had increased to a light rain.

Walking the streets of the dramatically changed zone, I noticed the faces of those who had been serving for the past ninety days. No smiles, no tears, just quiet stares waiting for the anticipated event of the day. Was it fatigue, weariness, or just a sign of the kind of day it would be? Usually by 8:30 A.M. all the heavy equipment was in full gear and the special units of fire and police had already been dispatched.

But on this day, there was a new sound: silence.

Workers were huddled together in bunches of two and three.

A street sweeper made a final pass, clearing the soot and ash from the place where we would all be gathering.

As the dignitaries took their places on the makeshift stage, we shifted into position, knowing it was time once again to pause and remember.

The bugler played, and the rain fell. Prayers were said. Words of thanks and appreciation were delivered.

Then, as quickly as we had assembled, we returned to the work.

Chapter Eleven

Full Circle

. . . I have forever been changed.

As I RELIVE THOSE DAYS and nights spent in the aftermath of September 11, I have hundreds if not thousands of images, moments experienced and people encountered, that float to the front of my mind with the slightest nudge. I know I will be processing their lessons for many years to come.

One moment, though, is always in the back of my mind, constantly, patiently waiting to be processed. During the remainder of my time in New York, my thoughts kept going back to this one moment, just as they do now.

On the first night we arrived, I had wondered why we had found ourselves going to Staten Island when ground zero was so near. I had thought the answer was Homeport's constant stream of firefighters who swept us along with them into ground zero. But I have come to understand that there might have been another reason, one that still has the power to take my breath away.

On the second night of our stay at Homeport, my team member Ryan and I had just finished a twelve-hour shift at ground zero. It was 2 A.M. in New York City. We were near the ferry and, since the night was wet and cold and the waters choppy, we passed up a ride back to Homeport on a small police boat in favor of the bigger Staten Island ferry.

On our way, we saw an elderly woman walking stiffly, slowly, down the dark, deserted streets. And beside her shuffled a small, dark-haired boy with an innocent, couch-potato look to him, perhaps ten or eleven years old, head down, sniffling back tears. They were both carrying full, black garbage bags.

Everything about the scene looked odd. An old woman and a young boy, in the middle of the night, walking down the streets of Lower Manhattan, carrying plastic bags. In normal times, I would have never spoken to them. After all my hours of working at ground zero, though, wearing my gear, my clergy collar, and my chaplain's helmet, talking to everyone seemed the order of the day. So we approached them.

"Can I help you with your bags, ma'am?" I asked, after introducing ourselves.

"Oh, thank you so much," she said.

"Where are you going?" I asked.

"Staten Island. We took the subway all the way from Brooklyn."

"If you don't mind my asking, why are you out at this time of the night?" I said. "It's cold, wet, and obviously not safe."

"Oh, you just won't believe it," she answered, sighing. "My daughter is a drug addict, and tonight she kicked him out of the house."

"Him?" I asked.

She pointed at the boy. "Him."

The boy hung his head even lower.

"She said he couldn't live with her anymore," the grand-mother went on. "She called me and told me to come get him, because she was going to put him out on the street."

My heart went out to the boy. He was probably carrying everything he owned in the world in that black garbage bag. This night was never going to leave him. His own mother was literally throwing him away.

So while my fellow chaplain encouraged the grandmother, I introduced myself to the boy. I put my arm around him and let him talk. His mother was having trouble with drugs, he said. He'd been in school only a couple of weeks ago in New Jersey but then she moved them to Brooklyn, and now she didn't want him anymore. And he didn't know where his father was. But, he said, it was going to be better now because he was finally going to his grandmother's.

The boy's words tumbled out. I wanted to offer him some tiny bit of hope and comfort. So I started telling him the story about a little boy, years ago, whose mother didn't want him, either, and had abandoned him. I told him how the boy almost died, and would have except for a sister about this boy's age. I told him how he had lived in New Jersey, too, and how he would move a long way away without knowing what truly happened. When I finished the story, I said, "You want to know what happened to that little boy when he grew up?"

The boy perked up. "Yeah, what happened?"

"That little boy is here in New York City. He has been at ground zero, helping people."

The little boy smiled for the first time. "Really?" he said, *"Really? He's here?"*

"Yes, he's right here," I said. "I'm that little boy."

The boy's eyes grew wide, and then he began to cry. I hugged him with all of my might. I told him that there would be many nights he would lay his head on his pillow and cry. He'd wonder how his mom could do this to him. He'd wonder what was wrong with him, what he had done, to make her quit loving him. I told him I knew because I had done that, too. And yet God had sent somebody just like him more than three thousand miles to bump into him in the middle of this one night of all nights. And if God would care enough to do that, then in the days to come, God would surely continue to send people to help him, if he would just keep looking.

We talked with the grandmother and the boy for a little longer, doing all we could to comfort them before we parted at the ferry.

As we moved to take our seats, my mind churning with both his story and mine, I prayed a small, silent, prayer: *Thanks for letting me, of all people, happen to be right here for this one little boy.*

And then a thought hit me so hard I stopped in my tracks:

Did I meet that boy for him—or for *me?*

Or for *both* of us?

I moved to the railing and gazed across the river, toward my birthplace. The shiver I felt was not from the cold or the rain. I had shared my story many times but never so close to "home"—in all the meanings that word implies. *Ray,* I thought, *you've come full circle. Look where you've been led.* Here I was, in the middle of the night, within sight of ground zero, happening to meet a boy, a mirror image of myself, who had nothing to do with the World Trade Center disaster . . . and yet everything to do with it. It was as if God were saying, *Look at what I can do. I want to redeem every part of this.*

So many people came to New York City after September 11, led there for many reasons, most of us following some inner compass. Whether I, Ray Giunta, was there would probably not have made a monumental difference in the big picture; others would certainly have done the same meaningful work I had had the chance to do. But whether I, Ray Lanigan, was there at 2 A.M., blocks from the site of that enormous disaster, to walk into the life of a small boy's disaster, did seem to make an incredible, stunning difference.

That, suddenly, seemed the deepest reason for why I had come to New York: I came for that little boy—and I also came for the man who once was that little boy.

"God, I don't know what the future holds," I heard myself saying, "but nothing is impossible with you, is it?"

I took a long look around me, memorizing the moment. Directly ahead of me were the shore lights of New Jersey. To my left was the Statue of Liberty illuminated in the night. To my right were the floodlights of ground zero. Everywhere I looked I saw light chasing the darkness. I had an overwhelming sense of all the human stories surrounding me. Each story full of darkness and light. Each story full of crises and turning points. Each story a matter of healing one heart at a time.

And through the loving reminder of a faithful God, that included my own.